Final Acts

SUNY series in Psychoanalysis and Culture
_____
Henry Sussman, editor

Final Acts

*Traversing the Fantasy in the
Modern Memoir*

Tom Ratekin

Published by
State University of New York Press, Albany

For information, contact State University of New York Press, Albany, NY
www.sunypress.edu

Production by Eileen Meehan
Marketing by Fran Keneston

Library of Congress Cataloging-in-Publication Data

Ratekin, Tom.
   Final acts : traversing the fantasy in the modern memoir / Tom Ratekin.
      p. cm. — (SUNY series in psychoanalysis and culture)
   Includes bibliographical references and index.
   ISBN 978-1-4384-2729-4 (alk. paper)
   1. Literature, Modern—Psychological aspects. 2. Autobiographical
memory in literature. 3. Terminally ill—Psychology. 4. Semiotics and
literature. 5. Authorship. I. State University of New York. II. Title.

PN56.P93R376 2009
809'.93353—dc22   2008047769

10 9 8 7 6 5 4 3 2 1

For my parents

It was a relief to have the illness unmasked, to have Death be openly present. It was a relief to get away from the tease and rank of imputed greatness and from the denial and attacks and from my own sense of things, of worldly reality and of literary reality—all of it.

—Harold Brodkey, *This Wild Darkness*

The only thing you know for sure is the present tense, and that nowness becomes so vivid to me that, almost in a perverse sort of way, I'm almost serene. You know, I can celebrate life.

—Dennis Potter, *Seeing the Blossom*

The virus produced a quiet space in all the hubbub, achieved a subtle alienation. Dame Perspective, the obsessive mistress. What dark shadows remain to be explored?

—Derek Jarman, *Modern Nature*

It was a disease that gave death time to live and its victims time to die, time to discover time, and in the end to discover life, so in a way those green monkeys of Africa had provided us with a brilliant modern invention.

—Hervé Guibert, *To the Friend Who Did Not Save My Life*

But there is a terrible clarity that comes from living with cancer that can be empowering if we do not turn aside from it. What more can they do to me? My time is limited, and this is so for each one of us. So how will the opposition reward me for my silences?

—Audre Lorde, *A Burst of Light*

Contents

Acknowledgments

For their valuable direction in the early stages of this project, I thank Rob Nixon, Marcellus Blount, Maire Jaanus, Chris Baswell, Anne McClintock, David Damrosch, and Julie Crawford. I also thank friends and colleagues who have been thoughtful and supportive in myriad ways: Margaret Vandenburg, Linn Cary Mehta, Ross Hamilton, Mary Gordon, Achsah Guibbory, Stella Deen, Nancy Johnson, Pauline Uchmanowicz, Walter Levy, Walter Raubicheck, and Sid Ray.

Finally, for their help in many different capacities, I am especially grateful to Loren Ratekin, Betty J. Ratekin, Diane Ratekin, Susan Krogmeier, Cassandra Ellis, Paul Vita, Jeff Tompkins, Vida P. Sobie, Stuart Brodsky, Robert Barry, Josh Lockwood, Jeff Reilly, Dimitri Jobert, and particularly Zali Win, whose support and encouragement made this book possible.

An earlier version of Chapter 2, "The Critical Process of Symptom to *Sinthome*: Allon White's 'Too Close to the Bone,' was first published as "Allon White Tracks Down Himself: Criticism as Autobiography in 'Too Close to the Bone' " in *The CEA Critic* 67:2 (Winter 2005): 62–75. Chapter 3, "Working through the Four Discourses: Gillian Rose and the Products of *Love's Work*," first appeared in *Prose Studies* 28:1 (April 2006): 74–96. Parts of Chapter 4, "Harold Brodkey's Traversal of Fiction: *This Wild Darkness* as *La Passe*," appeared in *The International Journal of the Humanities* 4:3 (2006): 55–61 as "The Burial of the Dead: Harold Brodkey's Traversal of Fiction."

CHAPTER 1

Finite and Infinite Games

Terminal Illness and the
Genre of the Literary Memoir

Changes in medicine, media, and mores in the last forty years have repositioned the discussion of illness in society. In particular, the emergence of AIDS, and its growth from what was thought to be an illness attacking only gay men to a widespread epidemic (although often considered a "manageable" disease for those with access to the right medications), has forced the public to look at the politics and social structures that shape our understanding of particular diseases. AIDS helped make the topics of medical research, health education, and sexual and racial stereotyping pressing issues, and in the process it placed the particulars of the disease and the people with it in the public eye. Although the symbol of illness as punishment perseveres, a greater openness toward the personal experience of disease complicates and diminishes that signification. The sophisticated discourses emerging out of this openness consequently suggest new ways of defining disease and new methods of narrating the stories of the ill.[1]

Because of the long gestation period of the HIV virus, medicine's increasing ability to treat HIV, and improvements in the treatment of cancer, many people are able to live quite long periods with these still-frightening diseases. The result is a body of writing perhaps unique in the history of literature. Although many artists have written under the burden of terminal disease, especially tuberculosis, never before has such candor emerged in speaking of illness, nor has such writing become so enmeshed in the political, cultural, and sexual issues of its day. In addition to creating works of art that include terminal

1

illness as a subject, many artists have written autobiographical pieces describing their own particular experience of disease. These texts address not only illness, but they also show how illness and creation interact, providing insight into how various genres (novel, poetry, essay, autobiography) are suited to convey different aspects of that experience. As a result, a new literary field has emerged in the last twenty years that addresses the reciprocal relation between the ill and disabled and their culture.

Such scholars as Anne Hunsaker Hawkins, G. Thomas Couser, Arthur Frank, Nancy K. Miller, Susanna Egan, Ross Chambers, and Sarah Brophy have outlined the terms and parameters of this new field, giving it a variety of names to reflect their particular emphases. Miller (1994) coined the term *autothanatography* to describe the proximity to death within autobiography, and Susanna Egan further develops the term in her 1999 study *Mirror Talk*. Anne Hunsaker Hawkins, a groundbreaker in the field, prefers the term *pathography*, which she defines as simply "an autobiographical or biographical narrative about an experience of illness" (1999, 229). G. Thomas Couser uses the term *autopathography* in his 1997 study, primarily because he is interested in issues of authorship and authority, and in the particular ways in which authors use writing to counter oppressive medical discourses or broader social stigmatization. And in *The Wounded Storyteller* (1995), Arthur Frank clearly summarizes what I see as the connection between these different projects by placing them in a postmodern context: "The postmodern experience of illness begins when ill people recognize that more is involved in their experiences than the medical story can tell" (6). Both medical and cultural narratives addressing illness and death reflect a loss of what Slavoj Žižek would call "symbolic efficiency"; they display a loss of belief in the traditional power structure's ability to provide meaning. As a result, individuals feel a need to tell their own stories, seeking "not to provide a map that can guide others" (Frank 1995, 17) but to serve as an example of how we all, when faced with mortality, must create our own maps.

Through this discussion I hope to show how these narratives of terminal illness are relevant to all of us. As Frank Kermode has written, "It is not expected of critics as it is of poets that they should help us to make sense of our lives; they are bound only to attempt the lesser feat of making sense of the ways we try to make sense of our lives" (1967, 3), and in these texts we see extremely focused efforts at making sense out of life. Of course, all individuals, because we are mortal, are in the same position as these authors. But for most of us, death is not persistently conscious. Absorbed with the elements of life—work, sex, family responsibilities, success, material goods—we allow the idea of death, of life outside of these signifying systems, only infrequent and fleeting expression, perhaps primarily in art and religious ceremonies. This avoidance contributes to both the otherness and the authority of these texts. As Mark Nash writes, "Because those who are dying are so close to us, and we know that we will follow in one way or another, that we are simply watching a time-lapse version of our own mortality reflected in others, these narratives have a particular poignancy and force" (1994, 97). How others cope with death exerts a strange fascination; thinking of death and illness may upset our routine, but we are always looking for a model that will make these certainties less frightening. Time, perspective, and reality are redefined when an end point comes into view, providing the writer of the memoir with an increased authority over his or her life story.

Many of the changes in tone and genre that are observable in late works support Walter Benjamin's assertion in "The Storyteller" of a connection between death and authority in narration:

> It is, however, characteristic that not only a man's knowledge or wisdom, but above all his real life—and this is the stuff that stories are made of—first assumes transmissible form at the moment of his death. Just as a sequence of images is set in motion inside a man as his life comes to an end—unfolding the views of himself under which he has encountered himself without being aware of it—suddenly in his expressions and looks the unforgettable emerges and imparts to everything that concerned him that authority which even the poorest wretch in dying possesses for the living around him. This authority is at the very source of the story. (1968, 94)

Just as the interpretation of a text is more credible if the interpreter has finished reading it, the interpretation of a life is deemed more valid if the author is aware of the means and time of his or her death. Benjamin suggests that the knowledge of death initiates a new awareness of self, because the significance of events in the subject's life story is now knowable. Moreover, he asserts that this awareness is outwardly visible and strengthens the knower's ability to convey experience.

In what follows I argue, however, that the understanding that these authors possess goes beyond a simple knowledge of the end of the story. Indeed, a common trait within terminal illness memoirs is the loss of interest in beginnings, endings, and the linear life plot. Prior to that discussion, however, it is important to recognize that the freedom and authority that come with an awareness of death present their own difficulties. The subject is still living and must interact with those who value the world's objects just as he or she previously did. Thus terminally ill artists find themselves in the unusual position of being caught in a continuous circle that asserts life and also acknowledges death, forced to maintain a precarious balance. The literary memoir emerges as a tool with which to achieve that balance in that the author translates into communicable terms the effects of an unrepresentable experience.

In her chapter on terminal illness memoirs in *Mirror Talk*, Egan provides an insightful overview of the thematic, aesthetic, and ethical issues raised by these texts. Indeed, I view two passages from her study as springboards for my own project in that she highlights the heightened intensity that appears after the terminal illness diagnosis and the subsequent disregard for linear plot structures. Egan explains, "Full awareness of mortality, from which most of us protect ourselves most of the time, generates a fullness of being to which these texts bear witness again and again" (1999, 199). She elaborates:

> They redeem their lifetime not by narrative, and certainly not by making sense or meaning out of their experience, but rather by a strenuous focus on illness, pain, and imminent death as crucial to the processes of that life. Their texts depend, accordingly, on strategies that deconstruct personal autonomy and continuity—strategies that mirror the unpredictable quality both of the lived experience and of life itself, reaffirming only the moment and that, too, only as process. Such strategies serve to express and to "realize," or make real, identities at the very point of demolition. (1999, 224)

Reading terminal illness memoirs in the 1990s, I was struck by the number of writers who experienced an added intensity to their lives and a fullness of being described in the epigraphs that begin this book. The intensity came not from the anticipation that life would soon end but from a new freedom: freedom from the fear of living. Indeed, frequently the proximity of death leads to the removal of a fear of death that manifests itself as our fear of "getting life wrong," or the fear of dying before we have "conquered" life in the proper fashion.

Therefore, here I take Egan's insight one step farther by analyzing more specifically the causes and effects of this "fullness of being," how they connect to the subjective demolition she describes, and how these insights might further our understanding of existence in general. In addition, I am interested in what these recent autobiographical writings can tell us about the impact of a consciousness of death on artistic production and the significance of the memoir as a genre. When faced with mortality, why do these authors turn to the memoir and away from their usual art forms? What kinds of knowledge or experience can the memoir convey that the novel, philosophy, film, and criticism cannot? In many texts written by the terminally ill, the sense of ending provokes a profound reevaluation of life and art and produces a desire to speak directly to the public. A consciousness of death can initiate forms of openness and change that provide significant insights into how one is indeed able to change one's life view, or "traverse the fantasy," as Jacques Lacan has described. Therefore, my approach will be primarily psychoanalytic, looking at the causes of particular mental states and how trauma, illness, and mortality affect structures of enjoyment and the objects and activities that give life meaning, always keeping in mind that meaning and enjoyment are produced in relation to established social structures.

Finite and Infinite Literary Games

I begin this discussion by introducing a tool that risks oversimplifying many of the issues at stake here. I believe, however, that its illustrative power justifies that risk. In 1986, philosopher and religious scholar James P. Carse (1986) published a small, epigrammatic book entitled *Finite and Infinite Games: A Vision of Life as Play and Possibility*. In his book Carse uses these two kinds of games in order to explain differences in human motivation in a diversity of fields, suggesting that desires can be better understood if we recognize exactly what kind of game the subject is playing. According to Carse, finite games are played to win, while infinite games are played to keep on playing. Thus the rules of a finite game remain fixed and lead to the establishment of a clear winner, while in the infinite game the rules change when a winner begins to emerge; the goal of the infinite game is to play, not to win. Of course, establishing a distinction between acts done for utilitarian gain (the finite game) and acts done out of a detached goodness (the infinite game) is not particularly new or original, but Carse's use of the "game" vocabulary highlights the everyday applicability of the distinction and connects it to theorizers of play in other fields, such as D. W. Winnicott in psychoanalysis and Hans Georg Gadamer in philosophy.

Carse, Winnicott, and Gadamer (and, as I will discuss later, Freud, Lacan, and Žižek) are all interested in how playing and games take the subject beyond itself, thereby determining particular trajectories of growth and change. They all show that the games we play significantly affect who we are as subjects. Winnicott's lasting legacy is his examination of the "transitional objects" with which children play and the "holding environments" in which play occurs. In "The Location of Cultural Experience" he extends his analysis of childhood play to adult life, contending that all cultural experience replicates the dynamic exchange between the individual psyche and the physical world. For Winnicott, art functions as a form of transitional object, something that is neither us nor completely other.[2] Similarly, Gadamer is interested in the ways in which play—also manifested in art and culture—diminishes the psychological extremes of, on the one hand, "subjective" isolation or, on the other, insignificance in the face of the "objective" (big) Other: "The structure of play absorbs the player into itself, and thus frees him from the burden of taking the initiative, which constitutes the actual strain of existence" (2004, 105).[3] Both Winnicott and Gadamer examine how play provides life with those moments that are most intense and most meaningful. Winnicott's claim that "This intermediate area of experience [the transitional] . . . constitutes the greater part of the infant's experience, and throughout life is retained in the intense experiencing that belongs to the arts and to religion and to imaginative living, and to creative scientific work" (1971, 14) is very similar to Gadamer's statement, that "the concept of the game becomes important, for absorption into the game is an ecstatic self-forgetting that is experienced not as a loss of self-possession, but as the free buoyancy of an elevation above oneself" (1976, 54–55). Both thinkers use the absorption of play to illustrate how the subject experiences pleasure beyond simply surviving or fulfilling social demands.

Carse also uses his two-game theory to show how games relieve some of the burdens of existence, but his primary interest is in how the finite and infinite games relieve this burden differently. One might say that the finite game provides security, while the infinite game provides flexibility, and in this way the two kinds of games reveal different approaches to living that are, in fact, determined by different conceptions of death. According to Carse, "What one wins in a finite game is a title" (1986, 19), and the title provides a kind of immortality. Once the title is won, it cannot be taken away: "What the winners of finite games achieve is not properly an after*life* but an after*world*, not continuing existence but continuing recognition of their titles" (22, emphases in original). By winning a title, one can use past accomplishments as security for the future; no matter what happens, one has gained that title and the consequent position in the symbolic structure.

Death for infinite players is more complicated and suggests a different conception of immortality. Carse connects infinite play to the consciousness and acceptance of death: "Infinite players die. Since the boundaries of death are always part of the play, the infinite player does not die at the end of play, but in the course of play" (1986, 24). But for infinite players, the game does not end with death. Carse characterizes the infinite point of view as one that conceives of existence as something that transcends the individual. When the infinite player dies, the game does not come to an end: "On the contrary, infinite players offer their death as a way of continuing the play. For that reason they do not play for their own life; they live for their own play. But since that play is always with others, it is evident that infinite players both live and die for the continuing life of others" (1986, 24). Clearly Carse's pamphlet privileges the infinite player and the infinite game, but he acknowledges that the infinite view is made up of many finite games, and that existence demands a kind of "self-veiling" in which we temporarily forget the finite nature of particular games. His point is that we "drop the veil and openly acknowledge, if only to ourselves, that we have freely chosen to face the world through a mask" (13); that is, he recommends that we accept that we have freely chosen to play the finite game, and that we acknowledge the often (but not always) limited significance of those games. In turn, this freely chosen participation in the game makes the game enjoyable and prevents it from becoming an agonizing, life-or-death test that only intensifies our fear of living. Winnicott also addresses the problematic nature of the finite game, finding that many psychological problems stem from an inability to play. Often his patients were so overwhelmed by anxiety, so in need of security, that they could not creatively enjoy the transitional object or facilitating environment. Carse's terminology shows that one way of conceiving of the goal of psychoanalysis is to change the patient's focus from the finite game (which is terrifying) to the infinite game (which is freeing).

I begin my use of Carse's terminology by looking at writing itself as a kind of game. Like the transitional object, the written text does not completely belong to either the author or society. The text provides a space for the author to play with personal ideas within a communicative framework established by a greater authority, a framework that enables the sharing of experiences between individuals. Winnicott explains that the transitional object occupies an intermediate space that is essential for the individual in that it provides what we might conceive of as a flexible "connecting zone" that negotiates the demands of subjective and objective worlds:

> The third part of the life of a human being, a part that we cannot ignore, is an intermediate area of *experiencing*, to which inner reality and external life both contribute. It is an area that is not challenged, because no claim is made on its behalf except that it shall exist as a resting-place for the individual engaged in the perpetual human task of keeping inner and outer reality separate yet interrelated. (1971, 2, emphasis in original)

Winnicott goes on to argue that this intermediate area is the place of shared illusions, inherent in art and religion, through which human beings naturally group together. Here Winnicott provides a useful insight into the pleasure of reading and the feeling we receive when we read a "kindred spirit," or what Emerson described in "Self-Reliance" as the excitement of reading an idea (illusion) that we ourselves have experienced but have not been able to properly formulate or understand.

In addition, in any quick survey of writers on the pleasures and pains of writing, we see feelings and intuitions similar to those described by Winnicott and Gadamer. In *Love's Work* (1995b), Gillian Rose describes writing as "that mix of discipline and miracle, which leaves you in control, even when what appears on the page has emerged from regions beyond your control" (59), which reiterates the *intermediary* aspect of writing: we have some control over how we play, but the rules of the game also control us. Other authors emphasize the role of negotiation necessary for mental health, as when Audre Lorde explains that "this was the first reason for my own writing, my need to say things I couldn't say otherwise when I couldn't find other poems to serve" (1984, 82). Lorde relieves the frustration of not seeing representations of herself in the culture by creating those images in works of poetry and memoir, thereby narrowing the gap between what Winnicott calls inner and outer experience. And, as a final example, Allon White illustrates Gadamer's description of being caught up in a game that frees him from some of the strains of existence:

> But weaving backwards and forwards between childhood
> memory and recollections of the unfinished fiction, under
> the duress of my present illness with its closeness of death,
> I unearth, here and there, bits of understanding and con-
> nectedness. It gives me a luxurious sense of indulgent self-
> archaeology. It also helps to keep me alive, like refusing
> to die because I haven't heard the end of the story. My
> Scheherezade. (1993, 35)

White's weaving metaphor gracefully illustrates the connective and
transitional aspect of writing, as he ties together past and present as
well as his individual memories and social reality. Understandably, the
Scheherezade image appears frequently in terminal illness memoirs
and shows how writing connects authors to something greater than
themselves. It is important to remember, however, that Scheherezade
is no ordinary storyteller. Her stories have no end, and as a result
she plays a kind of infinite game. Her story emphasizes that although
literary games are traditionally finite games, literature does provide
an infinite paradigm. Art and transitional objects can function within
both finite and infinite paradigms, but my argument here is that the
paradigm within the text radically affects the kind of pleasures provided by the text.

Art's ability to work within both finite and infinite games has,
historically, presented problems within debates on art's value and social
function. A particularly relevant example for my topic is Arlene Croce's
discussion of "victim art" in her 1994 *New Yorker* article "Discussing the
Undiscussable."[4] Croce laments what she feels as her exclusion from
choreographer Bill T. Jones's work *Still/Here* because of his inclusion
of the ill and dying in the production of this piece. Ross Chambers
explains that in creating this work, Jones

> organized what he called Survival Workshops across the
> United States, with people already sick or dying from a
> range of fatal diseases. He coached these people through
> a series of exercises in which they were asked to translate
> into gesture and movement the course of their lives, their
> image of the moment of their own future death. . . . But
> Jones and his company then retranslated these gestures
> to make movements, "phrasing" them into the more fluid
> movements and gestures of choreography. (2004, xiv)

Croce's complaint about *Still/Here* is that Jones has "crossed the line
between theatre and reality," and by crossing this line he has excluded

her, as a critic, from the theatre game: "My approach has been cut
off. By working dying people into his act, Jones is putting himself
beyond the reach of criticism" (1994, 54). Croce presents, in a somewhat
muddled fashion, T. S. Eliot's familiar argument that art should be
impersonal, and by incorporating even distantly personal elements into
the choreography Jones has violated this aesthetic rule. In her view,
Jones is producing not art but therapy or community activism.

The disinterested point of view, however, is not the most provocative element in the article. By holding the survivor workshops,
Jones was clearly interested in challenging the traditional parameters
of dance and the function of art, and therefore he would not disagree
with elements of Croce's reading. What is striking about Croce's article
is that, behind the screen of aesthetic objectivity, she conveys how
deeply offended she is (and her heightened language suggests that
this offense is personal) by Jones's alteration of these rules. Croce,
throughout her years in the powerful position as dance critic for *The
New Yorker*, has established standards for determining what is good
and bad, and clearly if others do not follow those rules (*Still/Here* sold
out the Brooklyn Academy and was an undeniable success) then she
loses power and, in fact, her job of deciding who wins and who gets
the title. Croce sees the critic's role as being of the utmost importance:
"Criticism had always been an issue in postmodern dance. I'm not
sure that criticism wasn't *the* issue" (1994, 58, emphasis in original);
"I do not remember a time when the critic has seemed more expend-
able than now" (60). One can imagine that in the long view held by
Jones's workshop participants, the critic is indeed unimportant, and
Croce's argument for the value of the finite game provides few reasons
to change that opinion.

Within her victim art article, Croce lets slip a partial awareness
of when the rules of the dance game changed and when she was left
behind: "The sixties, it turned out, had been not the golden dawn but
the twilight of American modern dance, and suddenly there was Pina
Bausch and Butoh. And AIDS" (1994, 58). Surprisingly, Croce does
not pick up the AIDS reference in the following paragraph. Placed in
a two-word sentence fragment, "AIDS" is dropped like a bomb and
then completely ignored, just as Croce chooses to ignore AIDS when it
comes to twentieth-century American dance. But the acronym explains,
at least for this reader, the dramatic changes in American dance that
seem to baffle Croce. One can easily imagine the devastating effect
of AIDS on the dance community and the inability of choreographers
to exclude that experience from their understanding of the body and
the role of movement. In short, the trauma of AIDS and the pervasive

experience of death inevitably changed dance, for artists such as Bill T. Jones, to a game with an infinite context.

If we look closely at *Still/Here*, its infinite qualities become even more apparent.[5] The work is, to a certain extent, about Jones's partner in life and dance, Arnie Zane, who is *still here* in ways that can only be understood from an "un-finite" point of view. But more than that, Chambers explains how the work's goal is to go beyond the comfortable conventions of form and structure to the personal experience of trauma:

> In so doing, he asked his audience (signaled them) to attend to a signified that "lay beyond" the threshold of the choreographed gestures, movements, groupings and images, the phrasings of dance ... something was being given to us as beyond the reach, precisely, of more conventional representations, as if the dancing was an extremely complex equivalent of one of those intrusive and untimely phone calls in the night that remind us of the reasons we have to be anxious but do not designate them. (2004, xxviii)

Chambers captures that opaque element within the work (one might call it an allusion to the Lacanian real) that evokes something beyond signification. Carse writes, "In infinite play one chooses to be mortal inasmuch as one always plays dramatically, that is, toward the open, toward the horizon, toward surprise, where nothing can be scripted. It is a kind of play that requires complete vulnerability" (1986, 25). This unscripted vulnerability is precisely what Chambers describes in the passage just cited, and it is also what angers Croce so much in "Discussing the Undiscussable."

So we see that admirers of Jones's work such as Chambers do not read it that differently from detractors such as Croce. They simply disagree on the value of Jones's use of an infinite point of view. For Croce, the finite game has clear rules, and following these rules draws out the best elements from the artist. By enforcing the rules, the critic plays an important function in producing worthwhile cultural products. In the infinite game, the rules change in order to avoid designating a clear winner. In Croce's view, if you make up the rules as you go along, then they cannot have much value. But we see that for Chambers this challenge to the rules is precisely what gives the work relevance and what relieves us from what he calls the "cultural dalmane" of the mass media. Croce wants the rules of dance to remain the same, and Jones is a problem to her because he will not leave things alone; he plays by his own rules.

Looking at the specific content of *Still/Here*, we see how that work's proximity to death nullifies its value for Croce. Death challenges the necessity of playing in itself and exposes the conventional and therefore limited meaning of the symbolic order: the world of titles and prizes. As Carse explains:

> Properly speaking, life and death as such are rarely the stakes of a finite game. What one wins is a title; and when the loser of a finite game is declared dead to further play, it is equivalent to declaring that person utterly without title—a person to whom no attention whatsoever need be given. Death, in finite play, is the triumph of the past over the future, a condition in which no surprise is possible." (1986, 20–21).

The presence of death exposes the insignificance of the title, and it is precisely the role of conveying titles (deciding "to whom no attention whatsoever need be given") that Croce embodies. Death puts an end to finite play because, within this vocabulary, "death" means the literal end. Within the vocabulary of the infinite game (in works such as *Still/Here*), "death" takes on a different meaning, signifying an unknowable space that marks the end of one phase and the beginning of another. For Croce, AIDS makes serious art meaningless, while for Jones, AIDS forces him to conceive of art and dance in new ways: to create new meanings.

Freud, "Death," and the Death Drive

I analyze Sigmund Freud's discussion of death in several different texts to support what I have introduced here as two different meanings of "death" that connect to two different forms of aesthetic pleasure. Freud addresses the psychological effects of death in such texts as *The Ego and the Id* (1960) and *Inhibitions, Symptoms, and Anxiety* (1959); in addition, the essays "The Disillusionment of the War" and "Our Attitude towards Death" (1915) (both in *Character and Culture*, 1963) address broader social responses to death. Generally, Freud represents death as another form of loss and links the fear of death to the fear of castration. He contends that we have metaphors that enable us to comprehend castration: "Castration can be pictured on the basis of the daily experience of the feces being separated from the body or on the basis of losing the mother's breast at weaning" (1959, 58). This metaphorical linking ties "castration" to the primal losses that humans are continually attempting to replace in their relations with other objects and people. If the loss of feces or the breast enables us to "picture" castration, then there must be a similarity to the forms of loss, even if they vary in degree.

However, in making the connection between castration and death, Freud's phrasing introduces an interesting problem:

> Nothing resembling death can ever have been experienced; or if it has, as in fainting, it has left no observable traces behind. I am therefore inclined to adhere to the view that the fear of death should be regarded as analogous to the fear of castration, and that the situation to which the ego is reacting is one of being abandoned by the protecting super-ego—the powers of destiny—so that it has no longer any safeguard against all the dangers that surround it. (1959, 58)

It seems that the fact that castration can be "pictured" while death cannot implies a difference and suggests that death and castration are not completely analogous. This does not necessarily mean that Freud's conclusion—that both death and castration suggest an abandonment by the superego—is false. The idea of death may evoke a sense of loss that one continually attempts to avoid or paper over. I believe the confusion lies in the two possible ways of interpreting the term *death*. On the one hand, death is an abstract concept that designates that unknown space beyond life (what I later explore as the Lacanian real). On the other, it is a specific experience that marks the end of life (an element of the symbolic). In the passage just cited, Freud moves from the idea of death that is unknowable to the death that can be experienced metaphorically. The first definition is unlike castration in that there is nothing after it—no diminished postdeath—it lies outside of time and space and is therefore similar to the infinite game. The second meaning is similar to castration in that it marks the end of life—a clearly finite life. To rephrase, I believe that a distinction needs to be made between a fear of death (the unknown) and a fear of dying (lacking life), and that what Freud actually addresses with the analogy of castration is a fear of dying. "Dying" suggests an abandonment by a protective force, while "death" suggests a completely different realm, a realm that evokes an odd form of pleasure, perhaps best explained by Freud himself as what lies beyond the pleasure principle: that which we cannot name but which continuously attracts us. This odd or unexpected pleasure frequently emerges in terminal illness memoirs and is, I contend, what gives them their intensity. But to understand how this pleasure brings both satisfaction and pain we must look closely at how Freud describes it in his later work.

Freud presented his much-debated and often-misunderstood concept of the death drive (or death instinct) in *Beyond the Pleasure Principle* (1961). This text developed out of his observation that many human actions could not be explained by adherence to either the pleasure principle or the reality principle. He noticed that people consistently repeated unsatisfying behaviors, and this repetition provided a clue as to how and why people make their own lives difficult.

Freud's interest in repetition led to his description of "Fort-Da," the game played by his grandson that has become the Ur-game for all psychoanalytic theorizing of play. "Fort-Da" is primarily thought of as the game in which the child throws a reel attached to a string over the side of the cot, yelling "fort" ("gone"), which he then retrieves by pulling the string and stating "da" ("there"). Freud points out, however, that this was an infrequent form of the game, and that "the first act, that of departure, was staged as a game in itself and far more frequently than the episode in its entirety, with its pleasurable ending" (1961, 9–10). Freud connects the child's playing of the game to the absence of the mother and sees the game as the great "cultural achievement" of instinctual renunciation, "which [the child] had made in allowing his mother to go away without protesting. He compensated himself for this, as it were, by himself staging the disappearance and return of the objects within his reach" (9). Freud's observation of this repetition of an apparently unpleasurable action (throwing away the object) leads him to a temporary dead end, however, because—as he explains—the repetition turns into pleasure through mastery, and therefore the actions still follow the pleasure principle.

In *Darwin's Worms* (2000), Adam Phillips provides further insight into the significance of "Fort-Da," and, as a result, he provides a path out of Freud's logical dead end. Phillips explains that in playing this game, "it is not as though the child is merely making a choice to manage his suffering, but rather that the mother's absence is an opportunity for the child to find another pleasure. And not only the ascetic pleasure of instinctual renunciation, but the pleasure of symbolization itself; the delight of making up the game" (121).[6] The creating and playing of the game engage the child in life and help him manage the universal anxiety that comes from being a human, without a clearly defined purpose or goal. The development of that new engagement *requires* the loss of an earlier pleasure, and Phillips shows how destruction and creation are, as a result, intertwined: two parts of the same drive moving life forward.[7]

This understanding of "Fort-Da" can now be placed back into Freud's conception of the death drive, which he hypothesizes as the instinct to return to inorganic matter. Freud suggests that we are driven by competing goals: the desire to return to stasis and complete rest, and the desire to increase living connections and pleasures, avoiding death at all costs. These competing goals create a constant tension for the subject:

> The tension which then arose in what had hitherto been an inanimate substance endeavoured to cancel itself out. In this way the first instinct came into being: the instinct to return to the inanimate state. . . . For a long time, perhaps, living substance was thus being constantly created afresh and easily dying, till decisive external influences altered in such a way as to oblige the still surviving substance to diverge ever more widely from its original course of life and to make ever more complicated *detours* before reaching its aim of death. These circuitous paths to death, faithfully kept to by conservative instincts, would thus present us today with the picture of the phenomena of life. (1961, 32–33, emphasis in original)

In this context, the game played by the child becomes one of the detours that distracts the child from loss and provides life with pleasure. We saw in White's description of writing as a Scheherezade experience a quite literal example of writing and memoir serving as a detour from death. What is particularly relevant here, however, is the different detours from which the subject may choose. In *Beyond the Pleasure Principle*, Freud makes the famous statement that "the organism wishes to die in its own fashion," but what exactly determines which fashion is one's own? One could argue that the "fashion" of one's life is determined in dynamic relation with the narratives presented and sanctioned by society. And we see in the terminal illness narratives I analyze (as well as in the culture at large) that these narratives often differ in their relation to what I am calling a finite or an infinite point of view.

Two *Sight and Sound* articles from June 1993 help exemplify how finite or infinite ideologies determine narrative approaches, and how those narrative approaches in turn manifest themselves in the cultural work on AIDS from the 1990s. First, Simon Watney's (1993) "The French Connection" attacks *Savage Nights* director Cyril Collard and French homosexuals in general for their lack of community activism and politicization in the face of the epidemic. Paul Julian Smith (1993) expands on Watney's observations in "Blue and the Outer Limits," in which he sets up a dichotomy between Continental and Anglo-American approaches to AIDS:

> While the Anglo-American approach to AIDS has been largely political (protesting against the injustice and ignorance of government policies), the French and southern European response has often been metaphysical (seeking release from pain in transcendence, in a universal love without limits). (Smith 1993, 18)

Smith's example describes in different terms what I have been calling the finite and infinite perspectives and has the added benefit of showing how we cannot automatically privilege the infinite perspective, as Carse tends to do. The political action attributed to Anglo-American society displays a need for factual understanding; it demands recognition by established power structures, and it foresees a cure for AIDS as the attainable and only meaningful prize. Perhaps best exemplified by the writings of Larry Kramer and Paul Monette, these "finite" writers seek to create support and political change through their writing in order to win a defined battle.

The French metaphysical response (with which Smith groups Derek Jarman's [1994a] *Blue*), perhaps best represented by Collard and Hervé Guibert, looks beyond practical solutions, attempting to fill the lack created by AIDS and the expectation of death by exploring new permutations of desire or being. At the end of *Savage Nights*, Collard writes: "The world isn't just something set down out there, beyond me; I belong to it, it's mine. I will probably die of AIDS, but this isn't my life any more; I am in life" (1993, 222). He suggests that he feels a connection to existence that will continue even after his death. Collard's movement outside of his life into the greater world (exemplified by the ocean, which is the backdrop for this scene) exhibits his embrace of the infinite, the transcendent, and the dissolution of the isolated "I."

Similarly, Monette's (1988, 1992) autobiographical work derives much of its power from his commitment to the present and his refusal of metaphysical comforts.[8] I am more interested, however, in the "Continental" approach, because I believe that the infinite view—a view focused on openness, surprise, and incompletion—reflects broader cultural developments, developments that are frequently called "postmodern." Moreover, I will argue in what follows that the memoir—that messy, unseemly, barely canonical genre—frequently operates according to rules that reflect the openness and improvisation of the infinite view. The rise of the memoir as a genre is, I suggest, connected to the increasing failure of traditional grand narratives to convince us that the finite game has meaning.[9] Forced by terminal illness to question the detours that have filled their lives, these authors must reconstruct their identities on an entirely new foundation, and the writing of the memoir is an integral step in negotiating between the past and present, the inner and the outer, to determine what is meaningful in this new context.

Lacan between Two Deaths

I finish laying my theoretical groundwork by translating some of the terms and issues I have discussed into Lacanian terminology, or "Lacanese," as Žižek has phrased it. The productivity of the Lacanian framework for this project becomes clear when we see how easily the discussion of finite and infinite games fits with Lacan's vocabulary. Lacan's division of experience into the three categories of symbolic, imaginary, and real is strikingly evident in Carse's discussion of games as well as Croce's views of art and dance. The finite view derives its power from what Lacan calls the symbolic order, that is, the social and signifying order governing culture. This is the world of prizes and titles. For example, you may be the fastest swimmer in the world, but unless the organization that governs competitive swimming gives you that title, you will not enter the record books and attain a lasting place in the world order.

In the early part of his career, Lacan emphasized the relationship between the imaginary and the symbolic orders. He presents the imaginary as the accumulation of images leading us to believe in a coherent, unified self. The psychoanalytic cure was originally imagined as the integration of imaginary elements into the symbolic order through the paternal metaphor, or law of the father. In his later work, however, Lacan emphasized "the real," that which predates or resists symbolization, and clearly the real is what the infinite player attempts to integrate into the game. As seen in Croce's comments, the finite player clings to the symbolic as all that is knowable or meaningful, which is why the rules cannot change. In contrast, the infinite player acknowledges the real and this is reflected in his or her willingness to alter the game. By changing the rules, the infinite player is looking for something more, driven by what Lacan will call interchangeably *jouissance, objet a,* or *das Ding.*

It is this constant striving for more that interests Lacan and leads him to reformulate Freud's death drive not as a desire for stasis but as the drive that will not let things be. Indeed, as Lacan presents it, the death drive is precisely that which is unkillable, that which insists that the game continue endlessly. This is why, for Lacan, death and life drives are really the same drive: "The distinction between the life drive and death drive is true inasmuch as it manifests two aspects of the drive" (1978, 257).

For my purposes here, Lacan's most useful application of the death drive appears in Seminar VII: *The Ethics of Psychoanalysis* (1992), in which he presents the concept of the "second death," "the one that you can still set your sights on once death has occurred" (294).[10] For Lacan, the death drive leads the subject past physical death to the realm between physical and "absolute" death. Lacan develops the concept of the second death through an analysis of Sophocles' play *Antigone,* focusing on what he calls the unusual beauty emanating from the heroine because of her position outside of society but not yet with the gods. This limbo position is referred to frequently by the terminally ill and is evoked in several memoir titles such as Monette's (1992) *Borrowed Time* and Brodkey's (1996) *This Wild Darkness.* But in focusing on the beauty possessed by Antigone in this realm, Lacan provides insight into my previously stated goal of determining how these texts acquire their intensity and what creates the particular "fullness of being" that they emanate.

In a way, the character of Antigone is a confusing vehicle for the concept of the second death. One might reasonably think that the first death is a symbolic death, what Antigone experiences because of her incestuous relationship to her father and her banishment from society. The second death would then be the physical death that follows, and the space between two deaths would be the action of the play. This obvious reading is, however, not what Lacan means. As stated earlier, the second death occurs *after* the physical death, and therefore it reflects a psychological state that is in fact detached from the symbolic order but that adopts what Lacan refers to as the Position of Last Judgment, the death that comes when all existence ends, and meaning is fixed absolutely. Slavoj Žižek explains that Lacan's concept implies a distinction between the two deaths: natural death, which is a part of the natural cycle of generation and corruption, of nature's continual transformation, and absolute death—the destruction, the eradication, of the cycle itself, which then liberates nature from its own laws and opens the way for the creation of new forms of life *ex nihilo*. (1989, 134)

Thus the zone of the second death resembles that of the infinite player, in that both assume that physical death is not the end. Furthermore, Lacan shows how the meaning of the infinite game also depends on this concept of the second death, of a moment when change will stop and retroactively fix meaning. Without the second death, infinite play also becomes meaningless.

Antigone is between the two deaths, in that she has lost interest in world of "goods" represented by Creon, but she envisions herself reuniting with her family's dead after her own physical demise. Her desire for death and reconnection with her family competes with more ordinary finite desires, but in the end, Antigone's infinite view wins out, and her beauty comes precisely from her connection to death, from her willingness to repudiate the symbolic order and "man's law." Thus according to Lacan, beauty comes from the ability of aesthetic form to provide a temporary proximity to death:

That is why I have tried to have you recognize it in our recent meetings in an aesthetic form, namely, that of the beautiful—it being precisely the function of the beautiful to reveal to us the site of man's relationship to his own death, and to reveal it to us only in a blinding flash. (1992, 295)

The proximity is only possible, however, when the goods of the finite game have been given up, or when they are understood as occupying a position with limited significance. Therefore, Antigone's physical death is not absolutely necessary for her beauty, nor is suicide the supreme ethical act, as some of Žižek's writings seem to convey. Antigone's beauty comes from her psychological awareness of her own mortality and her detachment from the finite games of the social world, an awareness and a detachment that she derives from the tragic events of her family. The play, like the terminal illness memoir, provides access to and protection from the absolute destruction of the relentless drive through its use of language. The language does not function monumentally to validate the symbolic order but instead alludes to a yearning that constantly destroys and recreates (Antigone's loss of status *enables* her to bury her brother), recognizing that no final end or final satisfaction exists.[11]

Lacan's Masterplot

One can imagine that for a critic such as Arlene Croce the proximity to death provided by a play such as *Antigone* bears no resemblance to the way death is included in Jones's work *Still/Here*. For Croce, the play's status as canonical drama and fiction protects it from the "bad taste" that would be proclaimed if a real incestuous family went on the road telling its story.[12] My point here is that Croce's taste does not coincide with a large number of current readers and viewers. The evidence suggests that audiences today can tolerate—and may even demand—a closer proximity to the traumatic real than Croce herself can endure. Of course, even with these new rules the real continues to be shielded by the protective cover of fantasy (no one claims that reality television is "real"), but one cannot help but think that a cultural shift has occurred to create the current public fascination with the real lives of other people.

In his influential essay "Freud's Masterplot," included in *Reading for the Plot* (1984), Peter Brooks argues, "It is rather the superimposition of the model of the functioning of the psychic apparatus on the functioning of the text that offers the possibility of psychoanalytic criticism" (112). Brooks's psychoanalytic criticism imposes the Freudian model of the psychic apparatus onto the nineteenth-century novel to explain how the novel engages the reader and provides pleasure. In fact, Brooks's method creates fascinating readings of novels by Dickens, Flaubert, and Conrad. But does the success of this method then imply that if a style or genre *no longer* gives pleasure, a particular psychic model has atrophied or been replaced? Does Croce's brain bind energy differently from someone born in the Internet age? Perhaps. But as Susan Winnett's response to "Freud's Masterplot" reveals, many different models, both within psychoanalysis and without, can produce insights into how and why we enjoy texts.[13] Indeed, my goal here is to show precisely how a different model provides different pleasures.

Therefore, in the rest of *Final Acts* I explore what the Lacanian model of psychic functioning, when superimposed on the late twentieth-century memoir, might tell us about the social function of these texts. How do they withhold or provide pleasure? I see the Lacanian model as being in no way the only useful approach to the memoir, but it does possess several characteristics that encourage this imposition. Primarily, Lacan's view of the subject emphasizes a continuous movement between what he calls alienation and separation, or meaning and being. This movement reveals the subject's need to destroy and recreate itself as often as necessary, and this recreation provides an interesting contrast to the Freudian plot with a proper end that the subject achieves through a series of detours. When Freud claims that "the organism wishes to die only in its own fashion" (1961, 33), he implies that if this proper death is achieved, then the organism has in some way "won" the game of life. Lacan, in contrast (and this is perhaps what is so disturbing about his thought), argues that the goal is not to win but to keep playing. In Lacanian analysis, the subject abandons defenses, experiences "subjective destitution," changes the rules, and, as a result, experiences new forms of enjoyment.

In Seminar XI: *The Four Fundamental Concepts of Psycho-Analysis* (1978), Lacan presents alienation and separation as the two processes that constitute the subject. Alienation is the result of the subject's contact with the Other, which Lacan defines as "the locus in which is situated the chain of the signifier that governs whatever may be made present of the subject—it is the field of that living being in which the subject has to appear" (203). The subject can only perceive himself or herself through language or some other signifying system, a system that dictates the subject's self-perceptions. For example, the subject emerges through a cut that separates the "I" of the speaking subject and the "I" of the subject of speech. Because the subject can never be fully present in speech ("I" cannot represent all aspects of the subject), the signifier functions "only to reduce the subject in question to being no more than a signifier, to petrify the subject in the same movement in which it calls the subject to function, to speak, as subject" (207). This petrifaction by language causes a lack of being in the subject, which Lacan calls *aphanisis*, or the fading of the subject.

Lacan presents this in a graph in which "being" (the subject) is represented by a circle on the left side, and "meaning" (the Other) is represented by a circle on the right. The two circles overlap slightly, creating a space he calls "non-meaning," which is eventually filled by the *objet a*, the object-cause of desire. The graph displays how the movement toward meaning diminishes being by representing the subject as one signifier for another, the unary and binary signifiers (S1~S2). At least two signifiers are needed to establish a structure of the Other ("I" acquires meaning because of its relation to "you"). Lacan summarizes the process of alienation as follows:

Let us illustrate this with what we are dealing with here,
namely, the being of the subject, that which is there beneath
the meaning. If we choose being, the subject disappears, it
eludes us, it falls into non-meaning. If we choose meaning,
the meaning survives only deprived of that part of non-
meaning that is, strictly speaking, that which constitutes
in the realization of the subject, the unconscious. In other
words, it is of the nature of this meaning, as it emerges
in the field of the Other, to be in a large part of its field,
eclipsed by the disappearance of being, induced by the
very function of the signifier. (1978, 211)

Thus no speaking subject can avoid alienation. By accepting the
conventions of speech, we lose a primordial fullness of being that
we will seek for the rest of our lives. But just as the signifier attenu-
ates the trauma of this loss (remember how "Fort-Da" compensates
for the absence of the mother), desire allows us to separate from the
alienating effect of the signifier.

For Lacan, the process of establishing being is called separation,
which, as Stephen Heath (1981) explains, carries several connotations:
"*separation*, a term stretched on the racks of equivocation and etymology
to mean not simply 'separation' but also 'to put on,' 'to parry,' and
'to engender'—how does the subject procure itself in the signifier?"
(83, emphasis in original). Lacan teaches that in separation the subject
looks for flaws in the signifier—the gaps in the signifying chain—in
which desire emerges and exposes the Other's lack:

That by which the subject finds the return way of the *vel* of
alienation is the operation I called, the other day, separation.
By separation, the subject finds, one might say, the weak
point of the primal dyad of the signifying articulation, insofar as it is alienating in essence. It is in the interval between
these two signifiers that resides the desire offered to the
mapping of the subject in the experience of the discourse
of the Other, of the first Other he has to deal with, let us
say, by way of illustration, the mother. It is insofar as his
desire is beyond or falls short of what she says, of what she
hints at, of what she brings out as meaning, it is insofar as
his desire is unknown, it is in this point of lack, that the
desire of the subject is constituted. (1978, 218–19)

Desire is the key to separation, because it is desire that will cause the subject to separate from the signifying chain. The subject looks behind the signifier, because meaning is never absolute: "She said X, but she meant Y." The subject of separation senses a lack and tries to fill it himself. Because that lack can never be completely fulfilled (outside of death), that attempt eventually fails, and Lacan calls the remainder produced by that failure the objet *a*: the object that promises an illusory wholeness and sustains the subject's engagement in this cycle. Thus alienation is linked to language and knowable, relatively stable ego certainties. Separation, in contrast, is linked to desire and remains elusive. Lacan's theory of alienation/separation has the advantage of suggesting how the terminally ill person continues to function in the world while at the same time relinquishing cathexes. It describes both the momentary need for symbolic representation (meaning) and the need to expand beyond that symbolization (being).

In addition, the texts I discuss here all exhibit Lacan's "further separation," or the traversing of fantasy, which Lacan links to the psychoanalytic cure. Within Lacan's *oeuvre* the cure is theorized in many different ways and is given different labels, several of which I explore in what follows. Anne Dunand (1995) explains many of these terms in "The End of Analysis II," describing the Pass, traversing or crossing the fantasy, identification with the symptom/sinthome, and destitution of the subject. In his own work, Fink has described this process of the cure as both a "further separation" and the movement from "desire to drive"[14]:

> The traversing of fantasy involves the subject's assumption of a new position with respect to the Other as language and the Other as desire. A move is made to invest or inhabit that which brought him or her into existence as split subject, to become that which causes him or her. There where it—the Other's discourse, ridden with the Other's desire—was, the subject is able to say "I." . . . This "further" separation consists in the temporally paradoxical move by the alienated subject to become his or her own cause, to come to be as subject in the place of the cause. (1995, 62)

Understanding, and illuminating, the traversal of the fantasy (or further separation) lies at the heart of my project, and I further explore this complex concept in what follows. For now, however, we might read the passage just cited as a description of the analysand's movement from object to subject. Freed from the desire to be the object that completes the other, the analysand is able to connect to enjoyment in new ways. Dunand explains that "When a subject reaches this boundary s/he can no longer ask him or herself what his or her analyst's desire is, but what range is left to his or her own desire" (1995, 255). Unfortunately, one might read Dunand's statement as suggesting that the cure entails choosing appropriate or satisfying objects instead of bad or dangerous objects. I believe that what Lacan means by "traversing the fantasy" is much broader and much more difficult.

For Lacan, to simply change the object of desire means still being caught up in the world of goods. The traversal of fantasy and the cure will require a confrontation with death that finally enables the subject to renounce that which has provided security in the past. As Lacan explains in Seminar VII,

> As I believe I have shown here in the sphere I have out-lined for you this year, the function of desire must remain in a fundamental relationship to death. The question I ask is this: shouldn't the true termination of an analysis—and by that I mean the kind that prepares you to become an analyst—in the end confront the one who undergoes it with the reality of the human condition? (1992, 303)

For Lacan, accepting one's mortality is a step toward the alteration of the premises on which all life decisions are made. An example of such a foundational change is the movement from the finite to the infinite view. For Lacan, the repetition compulsion continuously substitutes one object of desire for another, always imagining that the newly desired object will bring completion and fulfillment. The acceptance of death demands the recognition that no object will provide absolute security or immortality. This recognition allows us to accept the silly things that give us joy, identifying with our symptoms, playing for as long as we can.

In the analysis of my primary texts, I show how these memoirs lead to moments of enjoyment. One probable explanation for the plea-sure that readers in our postmodern therapeutic culture derive from memoirs, despite their nonlinear plots and inconclusive endings, is that the core structure of the memoir often parallels the psychoanalytic process. For example, using the standard markers of family, school, career, and geography, authors first describe their position in the world, or their alienation within the symbolic. Then they both describe and *enact* a separation from that position, using the memoir itself to place themselves within their own new master discourse. Therefore, the memoir's function as narrative entertainment (the internal narrative that, at times, resembles the novel) is supplemented by the writing of the memoir as an act in itself, the further separation. The subject presented at the end of the memoir is, in fact, not the same as the subject at the beginning, because the experience of writing has altered that subject. The blank page (or screen) facing the memoirist parallels the void embodied by the Lacanian analyst and produces the transformation experienced by the memoirist and vicariously by the reader. A central tenet of psychoanalysis is that the analysand does not simply retrieve memories but plays out for real something that did not exist before this contact with the analyst.[15] The memoir (like the analysand) does not simply recount past events. The author uses this discursive form to annul one identity through the establishment of an entirely new history. And, frequently, these texts follow a Lacanian ethics, moving from a finite desire that derives pleasure from a title or reward to an infinite perspective (an ethics of the drive) in which the world acquires beauty or terror in its own right, separate from egotistical needs.

This ethics of the drive (or real) has been an elusive element within the writings of both Lacan and Žižek.[16] I see my project not as a conclusive explanation of the movement from desire to drive but as an opportunity to glean insights from the pattern of destruction and recreation that emerges in the memoir, the psychoanalytic cure, and the experience of terminal illness. As many critics have observed, to traverse the fantasy as presented by some Lacanians is a frightening and rarely documented experience, but these unusual texts provide an opportunity to see that traversal enacted with an illuminating beauty that only comes in blinding flashes.

In a way I am arguing that Lacan's insight, particularly in Seminar VII, is both more practical and less innovative than many scholars have suggested. However, is not the production of this conclusion exactly what Lacan asked of his students and analysands? Lacan's circular statements and oracular speech created a fantasy image of him as the subject-supposed-to-know, the guarantor of knowledge and wisdom, which Lacan himself continually sabotaged. The opaque quality of his speech forces the reader to establish his or her own "good enough" reading, a reading that acknowledges and accepts the ways in which Lacan, and our reading of Lacan, is necessarily lacking.

CHAPTER 2

The Critical Process of Symptom to *Sinthome*

Allon White's "Too Close to the Bone"

Allon White is primarily known as a scholar and writer of literary criticism. He published two books, *The Uses of Obscurity* (1981), and, with Peter Stallybrass, *The Politics and Poetics of Transgression* (1986), as well as numerous journal articles. Born in 1951, White was diagnosed with leukemia at age thirty-four and died a little more than two years later. Of particular interest, however, is White's posthumously published autobiographical text "Too Close to the Bone: Fragments of an Autobiography."[1] Here White's critical eye turns toward himself and his own work, providing insight into the process of writing and the concerns and preoccupations of someone near death. In *The Uses of Obscurity*, White writes: "Novelists tend compulsively to return to moments and episodes which haunt or hurt them, but it is precisely this painfulness which coaxes forth their written elaborations and mis-remembrances" (1981, 3). In "Too Close to the Bone" we see that this process also applies to autobiography, as White dissects and describes the haunting memories that he feels compelled to understand. In this case, however, White is coaxed into written exploration by his leukemia diagnosis. The limited time he has left forces him to give up the safety of his familiar genre, literary criticism, and instigates a need to explore those emotional opacities present in his unfinished novel *Gifts*. Thus in "Too Close to the Bone," he applies his skill in literary criticism to his own novel to access those unconscious associations and patterns that have appeared throughout his life. For White, criticism as autobiography allows him to connect these opaque memories to his illness, shifting his attention from the works of others to his own life. His leukemia diagnosis has forced a change in the rules of the game, and the genre of autobiography enables White to keep playing. In this new game, he discovers that he has not been haunted by monsters but by the metonymic shifts of his own memory.

White's 1984 autobiographical fragment "Why Am I a Literary Critic?" is particularly useful in examining his attitudes toward language and writing and the pleasures or dangers that writing provides. White finds writing autobiography dangerous, because it lacks distance from his memories and his past. Autobiography focuses directly on those "obscure" moments or feelings, while criticism provides an indirect approach to those opacities, protecting the writer's inner kernel. Thus for White criticism provides protection through its rigid form and displacement of focus: "I am a critic because there in the writing out of the other the distance is perfect and I am safe" (1993, 59). White is drawn to the artists he analyzes, such as Francis Bacon (OH! how I understand those awful paintings!"[59]), because he feels he intuitively connects to their work, but he is able to explore the connecting element through the artist instead of himself, thus protecting himself from excessive scrutiny. For White, the "I" who writes criticism is a scholar speaking to other scholars whose subjectivity is eclipsed by the signifier and academic discourse.

This separation of the author Allon White from the subject Allon White echoes the split subject that Jacques Lacan (1978) describes both in the mirror stage and in the processes of alienation and separation presented in Seminar XI. The other, represented by the literary critic, appears coherent, organized, and unbothered by desire, while the self, the subject of disease and mortality, is a decentered being, never in complete control of his body, the past, or the future. Lacan presents in Seminar XI alienation as the result of the subject's contact with the big Other, which Lacan defines as "the locus in which is situated the chain of the signifier that governs whatever may be made present of the subject—it is the field of that living being in which the subject has to appear" (1978, 203). The subject can only perceive himself or herself through language or some other signifying system, a system that dictates the subject's self-perceptions. For example, the subject emerges through a cut that separates the "I" of the speaking subject and the "I" of the subject of speech. The signifier functions "only to reduce the subject in question to being no more than a signifier, to petrify the subject in the same movement in which it calls the subject to function, to speak, as subject" (1978, 207). This petrifaction by language causes a lack of being in the subject, which Lacan calls *aphanisis*, or the fading of the subject.

We see that this discussion of alienation and separation employs the metaphor of distance, a metaphor that is pervasive throughout White's work. Moving between alienation and separation entails maintaining the proper distance from a rigid, deadening structure and terrifying, anarchic desire. We see in White's commentaries that his decision to write criticism, fiction, or autobiography is tied to his need for protective distance from the real or his need to shore up a failing symbolic order. Particularly useful here is Slavoj Žižek's (1989) use of Lacan's concepts of alienation and separation in *The Sublime Object of Ideology*. For Žižek, the sublime object emerges out of the process of separation, as the object coated with jouissance will, hopefully, provide complete satisfaction. It fills the hole in the symbolic order. In Žižek's understanding of separation, the subject must pursue the sublime object, but he or she should not get too close to it, or the particular fantasy it evokes will be destroyed:

> That is why the real object is a sublime object in a strict Lacanian sense—an object which is just an embodiment of the lack in the Other, in the symbolic order. The sublime object is an object which cannot be approached too closely: if we get too near it, it loses its sublime features and becomes an ordinary vulgar object—it can persist only in an interspace, in an intermediate state, viewed from a certain perspective, half-seen. If we want to see it in the light of day, it changes into an everyday object, it dissipates itself, precisely because in itself it is nothing at all. (1989, 170)

For White, criticism provides this comfortable distance: "I am aware that this [writing], for me, is dangerous. It is all a matter of distance. Always I am underdistanced, too close to memory, too close to my past" (1993, 59). Only when traumatic events, such as his divorce or his cancer diagnosis, upset this protective distance does White risk looking closer at these objects of memory and desire. After the traumatic shift, he changes his position relative to the object by writing about it in a different way, in a different genre.

"Why Am I a Literary Critic?," published posthumously, reveals the importance of the sublime object in White's thought. As Žižek explains, "The sublime object is 'an object elevated to the level of *das Ding*'" (1989, 194), and the impenetrable Thing[2] is the focus of

White's attention in this brief, disorderly piece of writing: "How *close* now, how perilous the thing must be, the stamping of the beast upon the shore"[3] (59). Strung together in what seems a rush of panic, the sentences suggest a free-associative mind, self-ruled and beholden to no system. Punctuation is unsystematic; sentences run together. In addition, he evokes elements of mysticism ("For some reason, as I approach the age of three and thirty something is coming closer and closer to me out of my own past, and I know that I shall be a literary critic for very little longer.") and a discontent with the effects of language and the symbolic ("I have deadened myself with the last word. I killed my pain and my memory. I typed myself dead."). He knows he is on the verge of a new kind of writing but is unsure of where it will take him:

> Very strange that, even when I am writing on remote things there is a microdread at my finger's ends, a kind of reflex resistance which forestalls me as I go (it senses. "I" don't sense but "it" does) and it sends me off in another direction. I just had a sudden intimation of just how free I am doing this it really is infinite and I know that if I go on long enough then I shall have to meet it somewhere along the way and when "it" (what?) senses this it makes me stop. (1993, 60)

We see here that White is getting too close to the real, and his unconscious mind ("it") is protecting him from scrutinizing the particular fantasies that support his conception of reality. While writing this piece, White experiences the lack in the Other—the incompleteness of language—and begins the process of separation, which is evident in his sense of freedom and infinity. Certain memories and feelings evoke a desire for knowledge. In this example, the unconscious stops the process of separation, protecting White from the possibility that these memories refer to disturbing things but also protecting him from the possibility that these memories have no real significance, that they are simply fantasy constructions. White believes that if he writes in this haphazard way he will free himself from symbolic structures; he fails, however, because the microdread, the unconscious, is too powerful. Therefore, at this point, he maintains a "safe" distance from these essential memories.

The freedom that comes with the acknowledgment of the lack in meaning frightens White; it implies an asymbolia that he associates with hysteria: "I write, therefore along the inner edge of hysteria all the time without, up to now, ever knowing it. I remain this side of it by being a literary critic" (1993, 60). Embracing a genre of writing (criticism) that, more than any other, appears least directly evocative of the self, White is able to avoid the monster of memory. Criticism, however, prevents him from wrenching himself free: "And yet of course I know that unless I come to terms with those memories all is a mask, a screen" (60). This particular attempt at moving beyond the familiar fails, and White implies it is because he is unwilling to discard established structures and risk hysteria:

> I write to escape the memories even though by a slight deviation in rhythm or cadence I shall be suddenly stand-ing right next to them. . . . And whilst I am always looking over my own shoulder for praise and acclaim, I shall not be able to write one honest word, not one word of truth. It is hopeless. I am further away than ever. It has gone. I can conjure . . . nothing. (White 1993, 60–61)

Thus White groups the larger structures of academia with the gram-matical sentence in opposition to truth, and he ties the ability to reach his memories to magic, honesty, and truth. Starting out on the path of autobiography in this fragment, White makes progress but soon encounters a dead end. The obvious question this text poses is whether his quest for knowledge of the hidden depths is indeed necessary or ultimately futile. Is the force that is holding White back inhibiting him or protecting him?

We see here that, for White, literary criticism functions as a symptom. Within psychoanalysis, the symptom is a substitute or compromise formation generated by the unconscious; it is a method of satisfaction that protects us from the Thing or the lack in the Other. While it is popularly thought that the role of psychoanalysis is to remove symptoms, Lacan emphasized the necessity of the symptom and taught that the goal of analysis is to alter the analysand's rela-tionship to the symptom, as Colette Soler explains:

> There is no subject without a symptom, since the symptom signals an individual manner of confronting sexuality. It is through the symptom that everyone has access to his or her jouissance, supplying the lack proper to language via the forgeries of the unconscious. . . . One should not dream of eliminating it: an analysis which starts with the symptom will also end with the symptom—hopefully transformed. (Soler 2003, 90)

Lacan named this transformation of the symptom *le sinthome*, developed in his 1975–1976 seminar. The awkward neologism, *sinthome*, suggests several other terms, but it primarily adds *synth*, *saint*, and *homme* to the concept of symptom, thereby giving a sense of artificial self-creation to the concept. This shift reflects Lacan's belief that the symptom is not something that needs to be cured through articulation and integration but is instead something that must be consciously claimed and embraced to provide consistency to being. Lacan explains that while the symptom serves a necessary purpose, it also limits enjoyment, and that we tend to cling to our symptoms, even when they are no longer useful. In "Why Am I a Literary Critic?," White presents precisely that juncture where literary criticism is beginning to fail as a protective symptom in such statements as "I have also understood a kind of blocking to the flow of my writing and There is only the insubstantial smokescreen to my cowardice or my phobic drive" (1993, 60). At this point, however, the symptom maintains its hold, and this is explainable because White still *believes* in the symptom. Verhaeghe and Declercq differentiate between *identifying* with the symptom, which Lacan presents as the goal of psychoanalysis, and *believing* in the symptom: "To believe in the symptom is to believe in the existence of a final signifier, S2, to reveal the ultimate signification and sense of the S1. . . . Hence, such a belief in the symptom implies a belief in the Other" (1993, 67). White believes that if he can access the meaning of his haunting memories, then he will acquire an ultimate truth. Paradoxically, it is not until White relinquishes his belief in the power of that truth that he is able to access it, discovering that the Thing was indeed real, but that it acquired its sublimity from his own imagination.

Four years later, after two failed bone marrow transplants, White tries again to get at the real that refuses to be signified suggested by these opaque memories. Now, with the knowledge that he has limited time for the exploration, he is willing to separate from the protection of literary criticism and to reevaluate his own desire in the autobiographical essay "Too Close to the Bone," which includes an analysis of the unfinished novel *Gifts*.

White begins "Too Close to the Bone" by directly addressing the problem of genre:

> I suppose this is my biography, my life. Fragments of memory. Perhaps even a memorial. Except that I don't believe in biographies and advise you to be especially sceptical about this one, written, one has to say, under

the stress of illness and in extreme haste. Self-perception is distorted enough in the healthy; God knows what it is like in those gripped by terminal illness. Don't ask me: I'm terminally ill. (1993, 26)

White's ambivalence about the status of this text warns the reader that something unusual lies ahead. Although writing about himself, White prefers the term *biography* to the more common *autobiography*, thereby distancing the author from his subject, and this warning to the reader provides him with the freedom to write whatever comes. He accepts the distortions of his self-perceptions, realizing that they fulfill a particular need. The text serves as a memorial in that it documents memory and will exist beyond the life of its subject. It is not, however, a document of the facts or accomplishments of his life but a particular exploration of memory and desire from what appears to be an end point. "Too Close to the Bone" shows the preoccupations of a critic who is close to death ("Like beginning to write at twilight with no lamp as the darkness falls") and who is attempting, finally, to understand himself without the constraints of genre, praise, or objectivity. Comparing this text to "Why Am I a Literary Critic?," Jacqueline Rose notes, "At this level, the message seems to be clear: the critic hunts the writer because he is fleeing—but finally, will have to track down—himself" (1993, 180). White tracks himself using the critical tools with which he is familiar, as his search for understanding begins with the analysis of a novel he wrote in 1977, eleven years earlier. In this case, however, White's illness frees him from the constraints of formal genres and even objectivity. By stating "Don't ask me," he distances the text from broader cultural authority and instead roots it in the realm of the authority of personal experience.

Tentatively entitled *Gifts*, the novel was written while White was breaking up with his first wife, and White describes how the work of fiction emerged from a completely different process than his critical writing:

> One night I was in my room in Norwich (I had been teaching away from home at the University there) and, pained beyond endurance by the break-up, I suddenly began to write—*in extremis*, you might say (it seems it takes cataclysm to get me to write anything other than scholarly articles). I began to write fast and fluently, pages of the stuff, and though my eyes were full of tears and I normally write with pedantic self-consciousness, this time

> a coherent story sprang from the end of my pen already
> formed, the fictional names and the narrative all in place
> without my conscious mind having any idea that all this
> had been waiting inside me. (27)

Indeed, White incorporates into the novel details, such as the Ford
Foundation project, which he thought he was inventing but which
proved to be perfectly accurate. Unlike his distanced critical writings,
the unfinished novel is a product of the preconscious mind. White's
parenthetical remark about the need for cataclysm to write in a different
mode is very telling here. As we saw in "Why Am I a Literary Critic?,"
criticism keeps White safe from what is unknowable, whether we call
it the Thing, the monsters of memory, or the sublime object. However,
criticism fails to protect White when his sense of reality is attacked
by such circumstances as the failure of a marriage or the nearness of
death. Most people have moments when existence, as they have come
to perceive it, fails to make sense. Marriage does not provide a happy
life. Mortality was really there all along. When life as he imagined it
is shown to be false, it must be reconfigured in a new way, and this
autobiographical text provides White with a method to explore those
kernels that he sees as essential to understanding his new life.

The connections White draws between images and feelings can
be neither proven nor disproved, because they are the result not of
deduction but of his own associative mind. White uses autobiographical writing to create a holding environment in which he can explore
the connections between his memory and the symbolic structures that
have shaped him. His analysis of the fiction and his life presents a
writer who has adopted an infinite view in that he no longer looks
for a particular solution or outcome but instead enjoys the absorption of the process itself. As seen in the passage previously quoted,
White experiences a "luxurious sense of indulgent self-archeology"
by "weaving backwards and forwards between childhood memory
and recollections of the unfinished fiction" (35). Although writing
autobiography seems to postpone death, in that following the logic
of narrative one cannot die until the story is finished, White presents
himself in this text as someone who is, in Lacanian terms, between two
deaths. His opening statements and warnings to the reader emphasize
that his perspective is shaped by the nearness and certainty of death.
Therefore, autobiography also appears as a preparation for death and
a project propelled by a knowledge of death. White allows himself
the "indulgence" of self-exploration at this time, because there will be
no other, and in the process "bits" of connectedness are discovered,

although complete answers remain elusive. No longer afraid of what he will find (what could be worse than death?), White is freed from the earlier paralysis created by a search for wholeness, and he begins to claim his personal story as his life's work, thereby traversing previously sustaining fantasies.

The unfinished novel he analyzes is divided into two sections:

> One strand was set in the 17th century during the Civil War and concerned an obsessive, self-absorbed mystic called Nicodemus; the other strand was set in the late 1950s in Sardinia and concerned a hydraulic engineer called Lucas Arnow employed by the Ford Foundation to drain the malarial swamps of the Sardinian coast as part of the world-wide effort after the last war to eradicate malaria. (27)

The first section is more picaresque, with a variety of humorous characters, while the second becomes tragic as Lucas Arnow contracts malaria and dies. Particular images tie together the two parts: water, reeds, and the hydraulic engineering, which drains both the Great Fen that Nicodemus seeks and Arnow's Sardinian swamps. White is puzzled, however, by the distance between Nicodemus and Arnow and feels that some crucial knowledge is hidden behind that difference:

> Certainly, at the time, the two halves of the novel would not coalesce. They remained obdurately separate and opposed. It was the failure to integrate the two stories satisfactorily into one fiction which eventually prevented me from finishing it. Written in such rhapsodic haste, it just stayed as it was, resistant to any attempt at revision. Its incompleteness has haunted me ever since. Perhaps now, as I go on, I shall be able to finish with it. Finally. (32)

White finally integrates the two stories not on the level of internal narrative but through his own psyche. The marshes and fens of the novel evoke the moats and ponds of his own childhood, which were largely removed in the 1950s. White's sister, Carol, who was two years younger than he, drowned in a village pond at age three, and he asserts "that the death of my sister Carol was the secret kernel to my marshland fiction" (39). The novel is also shaped by memories of the family garage, Allon White & Son. The Bernoulli meter, the arrival of which may save Arnow, mirrored the many parts that never arrived on time at his father's garage. The engineer, represented by

Arnow, reminds White of the family profession he declined to follow. Finally, White traces the Italian aspects of the fiction to the Italians working in the garage, particularly Giuseppi (Jo), who took his own place as partner.

As White notes, the two main characters are astonishingly opposite, one a "visionary anarchist" and the other a "progressive rationalist." If we follow his assertion that the characters are "dissociated and egoistic bits of [himself] split by time and place" (28), what does their presence in this fiction and fragment of autobiography tell us about Allon White? "Why Am I a Literary Critic?" provides some insight: in that text he also attempts to find a balance between two poles, the criticism that separates him from exploration and the hysteria that limits his ability to function in society. In *Gifts*, Arnow and Nicodemus parallel these two positions. Nicodemus is the passionate fanatic, separated from the village and even his hangers-on when he finally reaches his destination of the Great Fen. Ignorant of the workings of drainage systems and dykes, he finds his marshland transformed into farms and therefore mystically disappeared. Because of his isolation from recent politics he does not know that the Lady Chapel in Ely Cathedral was destroyed, and he mistakes a broken statue for a sign from God. Nicodemus possessed mystical vision, but his vision lacks substance:

> Nicodemus does not recognize it for a statue, of course, ripped out from the Cathedral. He sees only the figure of Christ, and with this impoverished illusion (the Christ has only one arm and one eye, but Nicodemus does not notice this in his joy) the homely secular landscape of the new engineering is plunged back into a spurious Medieval enchantment. It is a moment of treacherous epiphany, at once plangent and ridiculous, returning the world briefly to the darkening, pathless wastelands of Nicodemus's curious vision. (29)

White's choice of language ("darkening, pathless wastelands") clearly signals his discontent with Nicodemus's kind of ecstasy. The epiphany without substance, like hysteria, reflects a dangerous separation from the world and, as a result, Nicodemus's subjective comedy turns subtly into tragedy.

White spends more time discussing the hero of the second half of the novel, Lucas Arnow. Although both characters may be a part of himself, he aligns himself more directly with Arnow, particularly in the linking of their diseases: malaria and leukemia. In analyzing/writing *Gifts*, White turns malaria into a metaphor. Arnow develops malaria not from mosquitoes but from his own personality:

> It is really within himself that the poison develops. His entirely laudable but quite limited petit-bourgeois sense of purpose and identity are no match for the miasmic forces welling up inside him. It is precisely the *absence* of magical vision and rage within him, or at least their deep and irrecoverable repression, which cankers his soul. (1993, 32, emphasis in original)

Thus Nicodemus has magical vision but lacks reason, and Arnow has an excess of reason but lacks vision. As White points out, Nicodemus's epiphany of madness parallels Arnow's physical death, showing the dangers of such extremes. But in one of only two passages from *Gifts* that White quotes, Arnow experiences the disintegration of his analytical tools in the process of dying. In what White refers to as "metaphors of communication," he depicts Arnow's movement away from systems of signification and toward disorder and nature:

> What was it, that crackle and interference which made everything so far away now. Lucas moved his head from side to side very slowly trying to clear his head filled with shapeless and indistinct noises. It was becoming so noisy, so busy. Like a city rush hour. So very noisy and busy. Then there was a final subsidence of all clarity and sharpness into a sea of unfathomable sounds, a voice receding just beyond intelligibility like a radio station fading away in the night. And it was getting louder. Lucas groaned in panic. Something seemed to split and slither deep within his belly. It's not silent not silent at all but loud. There was a rush of pure sound through the air like a wind becoming louder and louder crowding out and pushing him and over him. A gleeful confusion of bugs and babble tumbled and fell upon him like insects swarming in the darkness. Mosquitoes came, filling up his nose and his mouth until at last his mouth, stuffed with deafening noises, stiffened into a final rictus of defeat. (34)

I quote the passage at length to demonstrate how the style differs from White's other writing. The paragraph becomes a racing melee of narrative voices, alliteration, repetition, and other devices that express its freedom and inventiveness. Arnow's perfectly engineered world is drowned out by the inchoate forces of nature, just as criticism is being replaced by fiction. And it is no coincidence that he is in the situation of being drowned—by noise, water, or bugs—as this is White's ultimate fear, leading back to the death of his sister ("Drowning. The fear is of drowning." [1993, 60]). In addition to "drowning," the imagery repeats previous references to hysteria in "Why Am I a Literary Critic?," such as the "beast upon the shore" and the combination of letters that will "release it howling out of me." It is interesting to note that these images of hysteria appear at the moment of Arnow's death, as though White knows that being completely separated from meaning can only be experienced as death, when subjectivity is finally relinquished. Death becomes, paradoxically, the remedy to Arnow's "limit petit-bourgeois sense of purpose and identity." For Arnow, it is both release and torture.

The Bernoulli meter, the symbol of human invention able to prevent Arnow's death, and "the entropic degeneration of the earth," does not arrive in time to save him. Repeating Arnow's reasoning, White suggests that his inability to unite the two sections of the novel is tied to his leukemia. It is as if the novel, sprung from his unconscious, perfectly parallels aspects of his psyche. To finish with "it"—both the novel and his life—he must integrate the visionary mysticism of Nicodemus with the symbolic mastery of Arnow, and as these are both parts of himself, the fiction emerges as an attempt to unite these characteristics in "Allon White." If White is able to link the two sections through his autobiographical criticism, then the union would leave him without desire, thereby finishing his life. But the fragmented style of "Too Close to the Bone," signaled in its subtitle "Fragments of an Autobiography," reveals White's acceptance of lack, his transition to an infinite game, and the continuation of his desire. Although White has united the two plotlines in one text, the text itself remains unfinished, ending abruptly during a discussion of his father's garage, which allows a space for White to play as long as he is able.

The undercurrent throughout the autobiography is White's exploration of his illness, and he begins this search with his unfinished novel: "I know that a central knot of my life and unconscious world is tied up in that abortive fiction, but I cannot quite touch it myself. Perhaps the roots of my illness are there in that early attempt to write a novel. Certainly it now seems like it, years later" (27). By linking this spontaneous text to the repressed memories, White is able to analyze Nicodemus and Arnow and equate himself with them:

Malaria, leukaemia. My novelistic descriptions of Arnow's physical suffering were entirely fanciful at that time, purely imaginary. But since then I have lived through them all. And now, like him, I am dying of a terrible disease. But it is too late now, of course. Too late altogether. (30)

White's statement that it is "too late" now is striking. Does he mean to imply that his disease could have been avoided? And could it have been avoided by minding the lessons of Arnow? White posits a synthesis of alienation and separation, of Arnow and Nicodemus, that creates a complete whole, eliminates loss, and therefore suggests freedom from disease and mortality. In his final memoir, White connects his death to his own artistic failure. The paradox is that White is able to explore this split and attempt to unify it precisely because *it is too late*. The tension between these two elements is what constitutes Allon White as a subject, so to eliminate that tension would be a kind of death. The separation that he enacts in "Too Close to the Bone" is too late for Allon White the literary critic, but it comes at exactly the right time for Allon White the memoirist.

The exploration of the novel enacted in "Too Close to the Bone" is part of establishing a new subjectivity by constructing a new life narrative. Using the imagery of *Gifts* to rediscover his childhood, White eventually encounters his sister's death, the secret kernel to his marshland fiction. Thus his disease, represented by Arnow, springs from an identification with his sister:

In the early days of my leukaemia two years ago I was convinced that this death wish, this identification with my drowned sister, was responsible for my illness. Three things, tangled up together but separate, seemed involved. The first was identification: inside me somewhere Carol actually constituted a part of my being, she was me. Not as a part of my personality, but as something much more physical, an hysterical body, a violence which terrifies me even when expressed as mere words here on the page. (42)

But there is a second thing, a second way in which Carol's death is inside me—less exorbitant, a little more approachable, perhaps. I took upon myself, at the age of five, complete and sole responsibility for her death. (42)

> The third element in Carol's death was the childhood puzzle
> of death itself and my unresolved mourning for her sudden,
> permanent disappearance. (42–43)

Although all three explanations offer elements of interest, what is
perhaps more provocative is that White presents his illness as a death
wish without qualification. Clearly a form of satisfaction is gained
from discarding medical discourse and pursuing the psychological
and mystical. As I mentioned earlier, White feels that writing "Too
Close to the Bone" helps keep him alive, because he is unwilling to
finish the story of his own life. White's many speculations on the past
provide him with an activity that expands what is possible in his life,
both past and future. Perhaps the literary critic, who rejuvenates a
text by investing it with meaning, can perform the same rejuvenating
procedure on himself.

But I also would suggest that in this late stage of his illness, after
two failed bone-marrow transplants, White is quite willing to accept
an explanation that includes the fantastic. His acknowledgment of the
hysterical inside him suggests an embrace of a world beyond meaning and a need to understand his own feelings and desires. White
recounts his embracing of the mystical during his treatment for cancer.
His father had planted two juniper trees on either side of a garden
path when the twin girls, Carol and Debbie, were born. After Carol's
death, one tree was removed. Before his first bone-marrow transplant,
White planted a new tree where Carol's tree had been:

> My brother-in-law thought I was crazy, Debbie said she
> understood but had her doubts, my parents seemed to think
> that anything which helped was all right. So I planted the
> tree. I dug the hole in the earth, but before I put the tree
> into it I placed a small wooden box beneath the roots with
> a rose inside it and a short prayer to Carol asking her to
> help me. (44)

The contrast in attitudes between White and his healthy relatives is
both striking and understandable. Faced with a mysterious disease
and the expansive void of death, it is not surprising that White would
look for new symbolic forms with which to protect his life. It is as if
the mysterious operation of identification and its attendant hysteria
demand an equally mysterious symbolic operation to be eradicated. At
the same time, the ritual provides White with an element of control.
By performing some action, no matter how logically unsound, he is

participating in traditional structures of cause and effect that inform our views of illness and nature. Thus the crisis of health has forced White to blend ancient forms, such as the offering, with his individual symbolism and modern outlook. Pushed beyond what his family would call reason, White draws creatively from the cultural artifacts available to him to curb his own anxiety and despair.

Thus what haunts White in "Too Close to the Bone" is not only memory, as it was in both *Gifts* and "Why Am I a Literary Critic?," but illness. Illness, or the mystery of illness, becomes the part of the subject that is both internal and external, the key to his being, although separated from it, and it becomes the "symptom" through which all past events are interpreted. The text is driven by the search for this illness, so that leukemia becomes a master signifier—that which can be approached tangentially but never pinned down; leukemia presents a new kind of obscurity. White presents us with a chain of signifiers encircling death—leukemia, malaria, Carol, drowning, swamps, water—all of which work together through metonymic associations to evoke *and* to distance White from the absolute existence of death. The autobiographical text shows, however, that none of these terms offers the solution to White's illness or the meaning of his life. Their meaning and substance come from the way White plays with them, and as a result they are deprived of their sublime power. In fact, the sublime object within this text becomes Allon White himself who, by writing from this space between two deaths, separated from the "praise and acclaim" he described in "Why Am I a Literary Critic?," conveys an aura of honesty and directness that makes him a fascinating, if not culturally prominent, figure.

I finish this chapter by suggesting how White's text illustrates the movement from symptom to *sinthome* described by Lacan. My argument is that it is the text itself that enacts this movement. The autobiographical does not simply describe the past but functions as an act in itself, in that the writer takes his or her symptoms and inscribes them within his or her own narrative, contextualizing their meaning and separating from any possible subject supposed-to-know. The memoir is performative as well as constative and therefore evokes parallels to the end of analysis, as described by Lacan in Seminar XXIV: "In what does this sounding that is an analysis consist? Would it, or would it not be to identify with the symptom, albeit with every guarantee of a kind of distance? To know how to handle, to take care of, to manipulate . . . to know what to do with the symptom, that is the end of analysis" (qtd. in Verhaege and Declercq 2002, 65). In "Too Close to the Bone," White claims his symptoms, delineating their role in his life and his imagination. But he also shows his ability to manipulate them through the language of his text. He uses language to establish a new subject, a subject who gains *jouissance* from himself instead of the Other.

The desire of the Other is revealed by the screen images that White analyzes in this text. One could break it down by gender into two central desires, that of the mother and the father, but this strict division is perhaps more metaphorical than real. The desire of the father is explicit in White's text and involves his name and its connection to the family business, Allon White & Son:

> From long before my birth I was enchained in that *Allon White & Son* as thoroughly as young Paul in *Dombey & Son*. It was as if both the past and the future were already firmly in place, me to replace grandfather, my son to replace me in an endless, pre-ordained chain of signifiers. My prescribed destiny seemed written up on the housefront for all to see. (48)

Interestingly, it is not until White analyzes *Gifts* that he realizes the impact of his move into academia and away from the imagined desire of the father: "In retrospect, I see that this wrench away from my ascribed place in the chain of names was both more protracted and traumatic than I realized at the time" (48–49). The desire of the mother is less obvious and revolves around the death of his sister Carol. White explains his feelings of guilt after his sister's drowning and the resulting and continuous identification with her. It is probable that White, disturbed by "the anguished tears from [his] mother carried sobbing round to Grandma's house" (42), desired to fill the lack created by his sister's death, which would lead to imagining the substitution of himself for Carol. These feelings, that the wrong child had drowned, lead to White's belief that Carol can save him and the request to her enacted in the planting of the tree.

Near the end of Seminar XI, Lacan explains that the process of analysis involves acknowledging one's love for a specific object and then reducing that love to something mundane and manageable. He presents this in the phrase "I love you, but, *because inexplicably I love in you something more than you—the* object petit a—*I mutilate you*" (1978, 268, emphasis in original). In his autobiography, White acknowledges the powerful connection he has to the desires of his parents, but he also "mutilates" that connection. Putting the associations into language deflates their significance ("Last week it suddenly occurred to me as so obvious that it made me laugh out loud." [55]). The big Other determining his discourse is no longer cultural desire (literary criticism) or the desires of parental figures. Instead, it is the autobiographical writing itself, something White can own and, more significantly, something he enjoys doing. Verhaeghe and Declercq write that "Lacan invites everyone to follow Joyce's example and to create their own *sinthome* at the place of the lack of the Other; the aim of this creative act is to be able to function without the signifier of the Name-of-the-Father, that is, the Other" (2002, 75). This is precisely what White has accomplished with "Too Close to the Bone." He has filled the lack created by death with a creative act that enables him to enjoy existence in a new way. The text does not deny the void of death but plays in the space created by that void.

White's work stands as a powerful example of the preoccupations of the critic and the psychological demands of genre. At the same time, it shows how illness and writing can be only partially understood, even by the best critic. If the critic attempts to understand the essence of a text, then he or she is in the same position as White, who attempted to find the essence of his life as it related to his illness. That essence is, precisely, beyond language. And the tools of the critic, a (hopefully) orderly and coherent prose, are even more constricting than those available to the artist. Thus just as White's autobiography is called a fragment, any attempt to understand illness and writing is fragmentary—skewed by a number of interpretive structures, imaginary viewpoints, and unconscious desires that, paradoxically, invite the attempt in the first place.

CHAPTER 3

Working through the Four Discourses

Gillian Rose and the Products of Love's Work

In her autobiographical writing, British philosopher Gillian Rose evokes several qualities associated with one of literature's most discussed tragic heroes: Antigone. Antigone and Rose both present a detachment from the discourses that attempt to dominate them, asserting a freedom that appears both radical and exciting. In fact, in Book VII, *The Ethics of Psychoanalysis*, Jacques Lacan (1992) argues that Antigone possesses a particular beauty because she is "between two deaths," having suffered a symbolic death prior to her physical death so that she experiences the world with a detached, infinite view. A similar fascinating beauty is present in Rose's (1995b) autobiographical work, *Love's Work*, and the posthumously published (1999) collection of "descants," *Paradiso*. For Antigone as well as Rose, a meaningful life is created by connecting to individual desire, despite the judgment of the world. Satisfaction comes not from a perfect peace but from work and the feelings that develop out of risk and effort. For Rose, love emerges through a constant dialectic with desire and the lack that desire implies, not by protecting oneself with an imposed order or an imaginary wholeness. Rose and Antigone—heroines committed to ethics—enact their desire through agonistic engagement.

Rose's autobiographical writing provokes the same question posed by Allon White's: What knowledge and experience can the memoir convey that academic discourse cannot? And, like White, Rose's project is shaped by her cancer diagnosis. Given that she has a limited period to live and work, the memoir emerges as a response to that limitation. One could argue that every text documents the fulfillment of a particular desire. If it did not serve the author in some way, then it would not have been written. As Bruce Fink has pointed out, "A particular discourse facilitates certain things and hinders others, allows one to see certain things while blinding one to others" (1995, 130). This is particularly evident in the realm of genre, where an oversimplified example could be that poetry promotes interiority and hinders dialogue, while drama promotes dialogue and inhibits interiority. In his (1971) *The Theory of the Novel*, Georg Lukacs connects genre to psycho-social development, explaining the epic and novel in terms of integrated civilizations, with the novel emerging as the epic in a world "abandoned by God." One may conjecture that the type of integration that dominates modern consciousness is the integration of the self or subject. As traditional meta-narratives such as religion have waned, therapy and counseling have shifted the responsibility of happiness or utopia onto the individual. The memoir is the literary structure most suited to a society that accepts a radical split within the subject, because its central problematic is the exploration of that split as presented in the gap between the author and the protagonist. Whereas a traditional autobiography may be dominated by knowledge and ideals, the modern memoir explores unconscious desire and the lack within the subject. *Love's Work* is an excellent example of the modern memoir in that we see first the ideals Rose has been given, then the traumatic effect of illness on those ideals, and finally how she comes to terms with that trauma by creating her own master's discourse, or her own life philosophy. The immanence of death, which has forced Rose to surrender control of her body, also allows her to surrender control of her narrative, paradoxically separating her from philosophy as a fixed body of knowledge and connecting her to her own desire.

Rose's work provides another striking example of how the genre of memoir resembles the psychoanalytic process. Although autobiographical writing varies tremendously, the literary memoir that has become popular in the last twenty years is often structured around the psychoanalytic processes of alienation and separation. First, the author describes her position in the world, or her alienation in the symbolic or big Other. Then, the author describes, or in fact enacts, a separation from that position and places herself within her own discourse, finally traversing the fantasy that supported the original position in the symbolic. For a detailed understanding of this process, I use Lacan's four discourses as presented in Seminar XVII. As Mark Bracher (1993) explains, "These two processes [alienation and separation] can be seen as moving the analysand through the four structures of discourse identified by Lacan" (69). Thus Lacan's four discourses will help us understand in more detail what kinds of knowledge the modern literary memoir facilitates and what knowledge it hinders as the author traverses the fantasy in the writing of the text.

For Rose, terminal illness also plays a role in the movement through these discourses, as the traumatic recognition of mortality instigates the memoir and thus this particular form of separation. The threat to ego attachments presented by cancer allows one to view life, and one's life story, in a new way.[1] Therefore, in Rose's discourse, as in White's, aesthetic closure and the closure of a life intersect, providing a variation of Scheherezade's work: storytelling keeps one alive. However, the striking aspect of Rose's narrative is that she does not describe a diminishing of desire but an intensification that comes from a new freedom. Using Lacan's four discourses, I show how this freedom is achieved in stages (such as Elisabeth Kubler-Ross's more famous phases) that involve a negotiation with the desire of the Other and a final separation from that desire. Rose presents examples of all four discourses within her text, using primarily the discourse of the hysteric to demystify all that she deems inessential. She then uses the discourse of the analyst—that is, an act of subjective destitution—to lay the ground for the eventual establishment of a new master discourse that incorporates her failing body and her ever-present mortality.

Lacan presents the four discourses in Seminar XVII, *The Other Side of Psychoanalysis* (1969–1970). Bracher explains that in the four discourses, particular effects are produced, depending on the "roles or positions occupied in each discourse by four psychological factors—knowledge, ideals, self-division, and jouissance" (1993, 53). Lacan represents these factors with his own symbols: master signifiers are (S1), the network of signifiers or the system of knowledge is (S2), the Real that is excluded and produced by a system of knowledge is (*a*), and the divided subject, split between identity and desire, is ($) (53). Lacan places these four elements in a structure that resembles the multiplication of two fractions:

$$\frac{\text{Agent}}{\text{Truth}} \qquad \frac{\text{Other}}{\text{Product/Loss}}$$

The function of the agent determines the position of the other three representatives and thereby structures that particular discourse. For example, in the master's discourse, the agent is S1 (ideals); in the university discourse the agent is S2 (knowledge); in the hysteric's discourse

$ (the split subject) is the agent, and in the analyst's discourse the agent is *a* (jouissance). The four discourses are, of course, not exhaustive in their reduction of discourse to these four terms. They provide, however, a means of describing connections between the subject, language, desire, and the world that are particularly relevant to any discussion of the effect created by a language structure or genre.

University

Perhaps most familiar and therefore most easily grasped is the discourse of the university.[2] The best example of the university's discourse emerges in Rose's description of her experiences in school and as an undergraduate. Having already described her childhood inclination toward "Protestantism" and her belief in agonistic development, her disappointment with the rigid orthodoxy and unquestioned authority of these institutions comes as no surprise. Rose's impatience is palpable as she describes the study of philosophy at Oxford:

> It [school] did not prepare me for the deeper stupidity of reading philosophy at university. The oppressive opulence of Oxford was married to a vision of philosophy which would have induced in me a lifelong alienation from it, had I not already made the pact with my *daemon*. At St. Hilda's College, reading Philosophy, Politics, and Economics, I was taught philosophy by Jean Austin, the widow of the philosopher J. L. Austin. Jean Austin had published a paper on "The Meaning of Happiness," for which she was well qualified in her aura of tense dejection, chain-smoking with shaky hands, her nails stained orange with nicotine. A cramped, nervous figure, she received us in the spacious, slow sitting-room overlooking the river and the Botanical Gardens. "Remember, girls, all the philosophers you will read are much more intelligent than you are." The vacant, derogatory ethos of this initiation could not hide the contrary truth. Jean Austin did not think females could be trusted to read philosophy, to play the game. Hand-picked and super intelligent, they would either find the rules of the game fatuous, or *horribile dictu*, they might imagine that philosophy had some substance which exceeded the celebrated idea that certain kinds of propositions have illocutionary or perlocutionary force. "You do understand, philosophy has absolutely no use at all." (1995b, 129–30)

We see that in this description Rose is put in the position of the object *a*, receiver of the totalized and comprehensive system of knowledge represented by Oxford and, specifically, Jean Austin. The distance between this system of knowledge and Rose's own interest and desires creates a feeling of "alienation" in Rose (her word)—an estrangement between herself and the goals of the system. The details of Rose's description highlight her feelings of oppression within the university discourse. Rose implies that Austin's separateness from her scholarly subject—happiness—is both cause and effect of her own unhappiness, and the extra information about Austin's prominent husband and the luxurious rooms and grounds suggests a structure only interested in maintaining its power, not evaluating or rejuvenating it.

Rose's commentary makes clear that she felt there was no place for her own agency in this environment. The statements establishing the philosophers' superior intelligence and philosophy's uselessness oppressed her individuality and imagination. As presented by Rose, Austin's university discourse was a structure riddled with fear; the professor feared that if she educates her students, they will not play the game; that is, they will not reproduce the power structure exactly as it is. And Rose shows that this is a finite game that is, in fact, rigged; the canonical philosophers are the predetermined winners. Rose's description of Austin implies that despite her (perhaps tenuous) position as a winner within the university discourse, Austin is cut off from her own desire and, therefore, happiness.

Rose goes on to describe her frustration when attempting to connect the required reading (Hume) with a passion of her own (Diderot). "Pronounced perverse" and sent to rewrite the essay, Rose strung together passages from Hume and received praise for her unthinking repetition of the established discourse. Not content with this praise, however, Rose informs Austin that she is only playing the game: "If that's the best essay on Hume you've ever had, it's because Hume wrote it" (1995b, 130). Rose performs the dominant discourse but maintains her belief in her own intellectual curiosity and educational desires.

Master

In her description of her education at Oxford, Rose sets up an opposition between Jean Austin, who represents a "deeper stupidity," and Jean Floud, who saved Rose "from this pernicious nonsense" (1995b, 130). The example of Floud provides the reader with an image of a master's discourse that was satisfactory to Rose at one time. It is not the new master discourse she will present at the end of *Love's Work*, but in presenting this role model, Rose illustrates the elements of the dominant fantasy running through her life. Floud's attractiveness to Rose is encapsulated in Floud's statement: "How I dislike teaching undergraduates from the women's colleges. They will have been taught so badly." Rose writes that she "bloomed in this degradation, and knew that [she] had found "a kindred spirit" (130). Although Rose shows both Austin and Floud criticizing their students, she finds Floud's criticism inspiring, because it emphasizes the student's potential to fill, through work and good teaching, the lack she experiences. Floud acknowledges lack but acts to improve on it, whereas Austin presents the philosophical canon as absolute knowledge. Austin emphasizes tradition and idolatry, while Floud emphasizes the individual subject and work. This shift, from prioritizing the system of knowledge to specific knowledge within a system, reflects the movement from the discourse of the university to the discourse of the master.[3]

All knowledge, according to Lacan, begins as a discourse of mastery; master signifiers establish the parameters for a discourse or discipline. As a discipline, philosophy promotes a certain way of speaking and is therefore a particularly obvious example of the master's discourse. As Bracher points out, "Philosophical criticism—including even deconstruction, which criticizes the master signifiers of philosophy—finds it very difficult to escape becoming another master discourse, as demonstrated by the proliferation in the 1970s and early 1980s of deconstructive master signifiers like 'logocentric,' 'aporia,' and 'undecidability' (1993, 60). This is an argument Rose herself has used against deconstruction.[4] Yet her own discourse promotes potential master signifiers such as "broken middle," "activity beyond activity," and, as I will later discuss, "love's work," seeing in these terms an alternative to static theory or nihilistic despair. Therefore, in order for Rose to convey and promote her ideas, she must place them within an alternative body of knowledge that always risks becoming a new master's discourse. This paradox is the "tragedy of reason," with which all of her writing and thought wrestles.

In the preface to *Paradiso*, Howard Caygill provides a brief explanation of the difficulty of Rose's writing and places it within the narrative of her life:

> Gillian Rose enjoyed the reputation of being a difficult author. . . . Rose relished hearing stories from defeated readers of her first work, and would crown them with information that it began life as a commission to write a

cookery book. . . . The recourse to a difficult style did not arise from an incapacity to write clearly—as testified by the limpid essays that make up *Judaism and Modernity* (1993) and the posthumous *Mourning Becomes the Law* (1996)—but reflected the working through of the intrinsic difficulty of a "trauma within reason itself." (1999, 7)

Caygill's description implies that because she chose to make her philosophical writing difficult, Rose gained pleasure from alienating her readers. Difficulty emerges as an escape from the paradox of reason because it demands work, the active engagement of the reader in establishing meaning, therefore it will not allow these terms to accrue power separate from thought. Rose's solution in her philosophical writing is to accept the establishment of new master signifiers, but to counter their dominating effect by making the new signifiers abstract and difficult to penetrate or proliferate, thereby depriving them of their self-evident quality. We see in Caygill's comments and in the writing of *Love's Work* that this difficulty is something that Rose abandons when she learns that her life is ending. This shift, I believe, occurs because this original set of master signifiers is a reaction to the systemized discourse of philosophy—a finite game—while near the end of her life, Rose broadens her perspective and her audience, altering the rules of the game and hence her vocabulary. Confronted with the rhetoric of the medical establishment, New Age mysticism, and the self-help language of happiness, she is pushed into establishing a new master discourse that will counter the alienation that she and many others from different backgrounds experience from these seemingly totalitarian belief systems.

Hysteric

If, however, we agree with Caygill that *Love's Work* is Rose's "most difficult and esoteric act of indirect communication" (1999, 8), then how is this difficulty different from that found in her philosophy? And is the success of *Love's Work* related to or in spite of this difficulty? I suggest that *Love's Work* is a text, like Sophocles' *Antigone*, that is propelled by death and the sublime beauty of its heroine. The book's difficulty lies not in the style, although it contains its share of linguistic challenges, but in not providing familiar formulas for addressing trauma. This difficulty creates, paradoxically, its sublime quality or beauty, because Rose's unusual views and allocutions emerge as the result of a fiercely independent subjectivity. Like Antigone, Rose finds herself at the limit of the established discourses, and her sublimity comes from her refusal of the protection of these discourses and her willingness to experience exposure. Lacan shows how the limit and aesthetic beauty are connected in his discussion of Antigone: "The limit involved, the limit that it is essential to situate if a certain phenomenon is to emerge through reflection, is something I have called the phenomenon of the beautiful, it is something I have begun to define as the limit of the second death" (1992, 260).

Love's Work carries the subtitle "a reckoning with life," a phrase that implies the settling of accounts. The "reckoning" of *Love's Work* suggests Rose's challenge—to herself and her audience—to honestly evaluate how her actions have tallied up. The memoir thus becomes a test of her philosophical ideas through the example of her life, and it counters Jean Austin's assertion that philosophy has no use. The expectations of the subtitle are not completely fulfilled, however, in that a reckoning implies a final outcome, and this is precisely what Rose refuses to provide. In Rose's narrative, the reckoning becomes the point in and of itself, and she leaves the outcome to those uncomfortable with the broken middle, or those who insist on a permanent master's discourse and the illusion of wholeness. The process of reckoning, and therefore the text as act, becomes its own example of her project's worth.

In the *Theory of the Novel*, Lukacs laments the distance between "the conventionality of the objective world and the interiority of the subjective one" (1971, 70) and describes the novel as the attempt to fill that breach, the impossibility of which permeates the novel with irony.[5] Rose would agree with Lukacs's insistence on recognizing this separation, and she connects laments such as Lukacs's to the origin of philosophy:

> Philosophy, ancient and modern, is born out of this condition of sadness. Metaphysics, which, in Aristotle's technical terms, is concerned with the relation between the universal "nose," and the sheer snubness of a nose, which no term can capture, this remote-sounding metaphysics is the *perplexity*, the *aporia*, at how to find the path from the law of the concept to the peculiarity of each instance, from "the nose" to the snub. (1995b, 124, emphasis in original)

For Rose, the separation between the ideal and the specific is not a cause for despair but a motivation for further work and development.

Philosophy, as a process of mourning (and alternative to melancholia), "offers the consolation of reflection" (1995b, 125). Rose goes on to connect metaphysics, the "perception of the difficulty of the law," to ethics, the exploration of different routes on the way "towards the good enough justice" (124). And by positing this exploration as the highest good, Rose refines the gap between the ideal and specific as a foundational and integral aspect of the good. Her ability to accept the indefinite allows her to challenge the structures—linguistic, political, and cultural—that typically provide comfort, and to partake in a constant process of becoming, or what she calls the "work."

It is precisely Rose's ability to tolerate her own lack and her eagerness to challenge received wisdom that places much of her writing within the discourse of the hysteric.[6] Because the hysteric's discourse acknowledges the subject's split, it questions the master signifier and relies on desire; it is defined by Lacan as a step forward from the university and master's discourses. The term *hysteric* has quite another meaning from the colloquial or pejorative definition. As we have seen, for Rose, knowledge can only be produced from an acknowledgment of lack—from a recognition of failure or sadness. And since, according to Rose, the activity of the search for meaning is precisely what gives life meaning, lack is valorized and displayed, not papered over. Thus throughout *Love's Work*, lack, embodied in the split subject, becomes the agent.

Rose discusses her intimacy with lack most clearly in Chapter 4 of her memoir. Unlike Lukacs, Rose has no memory of a childhood ideal, a moment in which all desires were fulfilled. Proclaiming that she "was never an innocent child," Rose presents four "genies" who accompanied her and disturbed any possible mother-child unity: Immigration, Atheism, Divorce, and Dyslexia. Rose places dyslexia as her foremost disability, in that it taught her how to "germinate the other three." Learning to overcome dyslexia, she acquired a faith in her ability to overcome frustration through work.

Rose sees her dyslexia as more than a physical handicap. Indeed, she suspects that her dyslexia was "an unconscious rebellion against the law, the tradition of the fathers, and against the precipitous fortress of the family" (1995b, 37). Thus her childhood memories are of "Protestantism" against authority and the father, but they are not contrasted with a prelinguistic maternal unity. Within the larger text, Rose connects her dyslexia to her skepticism of the symbolic and symbolically anointed identity: "The confusion of names marks the child with the stigmata of the fantasised identity which he cannot assume—and so he stumbles against its central asylum, the written

names of the law" (37–38). As stigmata, the names represent what
Rose believes she should be, yet she constantly experiences her noncoincidence with these names. However, the working through of her
dyslexia establishes a paradigm of effort and reward that Rose repeats
throughout life and claims as her own particular method.

Rose learns through the work of reading that "the only paradises
cannot be those that are lost but those that are unlocked as a result of
coercion, reluctance, cajolery, and humiliation" (40). Reading functions
for Rose like a second mirror stage: "[Reading] became the repository
of my inner self-relation: the discovery, simultaneous with the suddenly sculpted and composed words, of distance from and deviousness
towards myself as well as others" (40). The mirror-stage child may feel
jubilant in anticipation of the unified being she sees in the mirror, but
for Rose the anticipation of unity is connected to work. Rose's dyslexia
prevents her from easily seeing a unified being in the language that
supposedly represents her. Any unity, in fact, comes from her own
effort, and this encumbers Rose with the responsibility of creating a
unified being, or of being personally accountable for closing the distance between her experience of self and that self's representation. The
name as master signifier does not have symbolic efficiency for Rose;
it lacks that one-to-one correspondence that supports the self-identical
ego. As a consequence, the responsibility to *create* meaning provides
Rose with the "incessant anxiety of autonomy" and the belief that she
could manage "the world to her own ends" (40).

Rose uses an anecdote to illustrate her complicated relationship to her own name. On her sixteenth birthday she discarded her
father's name, "Stone," and assumed her stepfather's name, "Rose."
She makes clear that even these names are simply substitutions, Stone
for the Polish-Jewish "Riddell," and "Rose" for the German-Jewish
"Rosenthal." Rose describes this as a symbolic act of self-assertion:
"[It] served as my bat mitzvah, my confirmation as daughter of the
law" (41). Rose attempted to make herself a daughter of the law, but
characteristically, she did it on her own terms. Beyond the symbolic
value of choosing her own lawful name, the change signified her
new ability to dictate the terms of her father's access, thereby sub-
verting his authority. In her act of self-assertion, however, Rose once
again is reminded of the limits of her power when she applies for a
passport under her new name. "I discovered, to my disgust . . . that
I was officially, in law, at the age of sixteen—worldly, voluptuous,
and scholarly as I fancied myself—an INFANT SPINSTER" (41). The
contrast between the fantasy of adulthood and control promised by
the acquisition of the name "Rose" and the government's subjugating

label "infant spinster" reminds Rose yet again of the failure of master signifiers (this time, "Rose") to encapsulate being and reinforces the not-all quality of any term. As in the hysteric's discourse, Rose's anecdote displays how the master signifier is lacking.

Another example of Rose's failure to find protection in language emerges with the death of her grandfather. Rose explains that as he lay dying, her grandfather lapsed into High German, "a language which, like all German products but German automobiles in particular, had been banned from [her] grandparent's house and presence since the war" (57). Building on the pleasure of turning seemingly impenetrable words into meaning that she discovered through dyslexia, Rose taught herself German by reading the philosophy of T. W. Adorno. She explains that she "was attracted by the ethical impulse of his thought, but also by the characteristics of his style, the most notoriously difficult sentence structure and the vocabulary full of *Fremdworter*" (58). Rose believed that the German language could be a "channel for [her] Protestantism against the broken promises of the mother-tongue," but it turned out that she was the only mourner to understand her grandfather in his last days. Paradoxically, her act of rebellion united her with her ancestral tradition, and her story exposes how the unconscious defines and structures what appears to be unequivocal law or meaning. In her grandfather's life, German was forbidden, but it appeared nevertheless. Similarly, German allowed Rose to exist outside of a tradition, both by experiencing her dyslexia daily in Adorno's texts and by acquiring a forbidden language. When the encounter with her grandfather occurred, she was forced to consider to what extent her learning of German was an unconscious desire, perhaps a desire to return to a repressed element of her family heritage.

These examples show how Rose's deliberate efforts to live her life in a particular way were shaped and redefined by forces beyond her control, or, in Lacan's phrase, they show how "desire is the desire of the Other." As is typical for the modern memoir, Rose structures her text around those opaque moments when logic or reason fails or is diverted by the emergence of desire. Those failures, however, are not melancholy or tragic for Rose. Within the memoir, each failure offers a new opportunity for reflection and knowledge in the same way that sadness spurs philosophic thought. Bruce Fink writes that "knowledge is perhaps eroticized to a greater extent in the hysteric's discourse than elsewhere" (1995, 133), and he does not mean the kind of knowledge that explains "how things are," which simply reproduces power, as in the university and master discourses. The hysteric's knowledge of lack as presented by Rose questions orthodoxy and thereby challenges stagnation. Knowledge is not an answer but "a process of learning, the corrigibility of experience" (1995b, 127). And it is erotic because it evokes and promises a fulfillment beyond the present. It promises a lost or, more specifically, a yet-to-be-discovered, object of satisfaction.

One of Rose's most challenging anecdotes describes her connection to her Hasidic neighbors in Stoke Newington. Originally Rose did not realize that she was living in a Hasidic community, but over time she not only discovered this but partially assimilated into the neighborhood: "On those days when, my own hair unwashed, I dashed to the launderette in the local parade of shops, with a chiffon scarf covering my head, my face scrubbed and unmade-up, I would be greeted and treated as a member" (43). Rose finally recognized how accustomed she had become to the neighborhood when she saw an ordinary English wedding party arrive across the street:

> What struck me at once was the lightness of the vision: slender young bridesmaids in short white muslin dresses with loose bare limbs, the adults attired in the pastel hues of matrimonial finery, and the commingling of the sexes in easy high spirits, all on their way from the church ceremony to the jollifications of the reception. (1995b, 44)

Rose's apparent pleasure in this familiar spectacle is undercut, however, by an irrational response; her body responds physically to the exposed lack in the Other that the conflicting cultures create:

> My disinterested perception of this happy procession was brusquely interrupted by the loud irruption of a subhuman howling, the source of which was unlocatable. It was howling as if from a dark, dank cave, where some deformed brute had been chained and tempted since time immemorial. The howling did not cease even after the last of the wedding party had disappeared from view.
>
> It was I who was howling, in utter disassociation from myself, the paroxysm provoked by the vivacious contrast between the environing Judaism and this epiphany of Protestants, the customary, laborious everydayness broken by the moment of marriage, the cloaks of the clandestine pious cleaved by the costumes of those weightless, redeemed beings. To this day, I cannot go to family weddings. (1995b, 44–45)

This passage establishes several apparent contradictions, beginning with the reader's traditional expectation that the author present herself as a coherent, unified subject. Within the memoir, Rose makes her persona just as vulnerable to lack and fallibility as the authority figures she exposes. This particular cut in the smooth surface of Rose's narrator, however, is provoked by the competing representations of pleasure represented by Hasidic Judaism and secularized Protestantism. The appearance of the light, modern, sexual Protestants in the heavily clothed Hasidic neighborhood functions as a metaphorical stripping of the signifier, revealing that underneath both clandestine piety and stylish beauty nothing exists but social convention, and the "howling" conveys the physical, animal response to this momentary emergence of emptiness when the phantasmic support has been negated.

Rose's intellect can interpret the signs of both cultures, but her unconscious, perhaps responding to the competing and therefore unfulfillable demands of the particular fantasies presented (heaviness, law, and tradition for the Hasidic community; lightness, pleasure, and the modern for the Christians), reacts with an unsymbolizable, physical symptom, which evokes the discourse of the hysteric as explained by Fink: "The hysteric maintains the primacy of subjective division, the contradiction between conscious and unconscious, and thus the conflictual, or self-contradictory, nature of desire itself" (1995, 133). Rose's response to the Protestant wedding party reminds us that despite culture's best attempts to naturalize sacraments such as marriage, a wedding is much more than a routine ceremony. Weddings not only enact the allowable channels for desire and fulfillment, they sanctify those channels, thereby implicitly devaluing other alternatives. In this scenario, Rose's dialectic of Judaism and Protestantism is unable to find a synthesis. Assimilated to the everyday labor of her neighborhood and attracted to the lightness of the visitors, she recognizes the artificiality of both, and hence the denial demanded in the fulfillment of their mutual promises. It is precisely the common belief in the wedding as a site of unequivocal, unquestionable happiness that makes it a horrifying experience for the nonbeliever. The naïve expectations of the wedding as sacrament or, more colloquially, "the happiest day of one's life" do indeed have a tragic quality when placed in a discourse that throws doubt on the phantasmic support of such meaning.

Analyst

Bracher summarizes the aim of analysis as helping "the patient encounter, acknowledge, identify, and finally come to identify with this excluded part of his or her being, the *a*" (1993, 69). And the analysand participates in this activity because of a disturbance, a disturbance analysis explains as a "conflict between, on the one hand, the identity (the S1) the patient has assumed and tries to maintain, and, on the other hand, an unconscious desire for jouissance (the *a*) that is, excentric to or incommensurable with (i.e., forbidden by) this assumed identity" (69). I suggest that the writing of the memoir is similar to the working through of analysis in that through writing Rose hopes to identify the cause of the dissociation and then integrate the new understanding into her definition of her own identity. Just as she was able, through work, to make the jumbled dyslexic letters yield to the broader language, through the work of thought and writing she will place her symptom in a greater linguistic frame and thereby endow it with a more acceptable meaning.

Therefore, we see that the memoir is not simply a description of past events but an interrogation by the speaking subject (author) of the subject of the statement (protagonist). In taking one's self as subject matter, the memoirist founds his or her activity on a split or cut between a conception of self and the failure to coincide with that self. Thus the modern memoir typically takes as its subject not the failure of government, society, or a broader symbolic frame but the failure or gap, that within the individual and the response to that gap, is, according to Lacan, the subject. As Slavoj Žižek explains:

> . . . a symbolic field is always and by definition in itself "decentered," structured around a central void/impossibility (a personal life-narrative, say, is a *bricolage* of ultimately failed attempts to come to terms with some trauma; a social edifice is an ultimately failed attempt to displace/obfuscate its constitutive antagonism); and an act disturbs the symbolic field into which it intervenes not out of nowhere, but precisely *from the standpoint of this inherent impossibility, stumbling block, which is its hidden, disavowed structuring principle.* (2000, 125, emphases in original)

Within *Love's Work* the reader follows as Rose explores the experience of her own void/impossibility. She identifies or "maps" the master signifiers (e.g., Judaism, Protestantism) that create the conflict and then uses language to understand and partially reconcile that conflict. Within the vocabulary of alienation and separation presented by Lacan (1978) in Seminar XI, the mapping enacts alienation, and the reconfiguring displays separation. According to Lacan, it is through the analyst's discourse

$$\frac{a}{S2} \qquad \frac{\$}{S1}$$

that separation is completed. In the analyst's discourse, object *a, jouissance* or the cause of desire, is the agent, and this desire questions or interrogates the subject's division ($) as exhibited in "cracks" or symptoms. This questioning forces the split subject to work to produce connections and produce a new master signifier. This master signifier is superior to the previous ones in that it has been questioned and owned, that is, the subject takes responsibility for it, resulting in an altered sense of identity and, as Rose (1996) emphasizes in *Mourning Becomes the Law*, a strengthened understanding of values and ethics.

The similarity between the analytic process, Lacan's four discourses, and the structure of the memoir can help us understand the attraction so many people currently have to this genre. If we add current elaborations on Lacan's concept of the act by Žižek, then we see that the structure of the memoir parallels the four discourses and also takes the act as its central problematic. In his work, Žižek shows how the act enables change—change in the fundamental fantasy that grounds the subject, and change that in turn enables the subject to alter the symbolic.[7] Within the four discourses, the act corresponds to the discourse of the analyst in that both remove the subject from the repetition of familiar patterns by placing lack in the position of the agent. In "Four Discourses, Four Subjects," Žižek explains the discourse of the analyst:

> . . . the agent (analyst) reduces himself to the void that provokes the subject into confronting the truth of his desire. Knowledge in the position of "truth" below the bar under the "agent," of course, refers to the supposed knowledge of the analyst, and, simultaneously, signals that the knowledge gained here will not be the neutral "objective" knowledge of scientific adequacy, but the knowledge that concerns the subject (analysand) in the truth of his subjective position. What this discourse "produces" is then the Master-Signifier (i.e., the unconscious "sinthome"), the cipher of enjoyment, to which the subject was unknowingly subjected. (1998, 80)

One captivating aspect of the memoir is that its function as narrative entertainment (the internal narrative that resembles the novel) is supplemented by writing of the memoir as an act in itself. The memoir performs the discourse of the analyst on a level initially separated from the diegesis of the memoir but eventually reincorporated back into the narrative as the new master signifier. Susan Griffin has explained this performative experience of memoir writing: "What is so astonishing about putting one's life into words, about telling a story, is that certain aspects of being are not only revealed but come to exist fully for the first time" (1992, 358). The subject presented at the end of the memoir is not the same as the subject at the beginning, because the experience of writing has altered that subject. The blank page (or screen) facing the memoirist parallels the void embodied by the Lacanian analyst and produces the transference experienced by the memoirist and the subject within the analyst's discourse. This is clearly summarized by Rex Butler:

> For Žižek, it is just his emphasis on the material presence of the analyst that also characterizes psychoanalysis, and why that "trauma" it diagnoses is not merely to be understood as some repressed and timeless memory the analyst helps us to recover but as something that is played out for real within the psychoanalytic session, something that *does not exist* before analysis and actual contacts with the analyst (2005, 20, emphasis added)

The memoir (like the analysand) does not simply recount past events. It annuls the identity of the subject in such a way that he or she uses these discursive forms to establish a history that did not previously exist. In both cases, this alternative adds a piece of the real to the previously accepted discourse, simultaneously unmasking the previous master's discourse—destroying its aura—but turning the new object, and the new subject, into a sublime object through this supplement.[8]

Rose illustrates her individual process of identifying with her symptom by narrating her reaction to an affair that she had with a priest. It is a great tabloid story, replete with voyeuristic value, but Rose never uses that discourse. Her language remains abstract and metaphorical as she attempts to describe and understand her own desire. Specific actions and events only appear as they illuminate that desire. Rose chooses this story because it fits a common pattern: "Someone who seems free may turn out to be encumbered," and, as a result, "the Beloved is bereft of the Lover; she must become the Lover: she must generate love but without the love she received" (1995b, 71). This shift from beloved to lover provides a first step in separating from the desire of the other. Bereft of the lover, Rose can no longer respond to the *che vuoi?* (What do you want from me?) that he presented. The love she generates cannot be a response to the lover's fantasy of her but instead must come from herself. Removing the lover's fantasy of her is a first step in the stripping of self that Rose enacts when she adopts the discourse of the analyst within *Love's Work*.

She must, in order to comprehend her reaction to the failed love affair, evaluate the meaning of "love" itself and what kind of expectations and beliefs she brings to it, just as her previous discourse questioned the meaning of "wedding." The discourse of philosophy, another support to which she habitually turns, offers no consolation:

> Why is it so agonising to the Beloved when the Lover wards off love? The answer "loss" repeats the question. This conversion out of love, its incompletion, is the illimitable medium of this whole composition. It is the point at which lovelessness confesses that she is investigating herself. Can this be sound method? Sheridan said of Scholasticus that he wanted to learn to swim without entering the water. Here, the method must be circular, and that is why it is not vitiated. Well, I am immersed. But if I am floundering, can I be saved by thrashing around? (1995b, 72)

The agony Rose describes is precisely what establishes the fullness of love separated from the phantasmic support of knowledge. Lack of completion, or loss, exposes desire that had previously been protected or papered over by the imaginary aspect of the affair. For Rose to understand that desire, she must experience it; she must jump in the water not knowing if she will swim or drown. If she does not, then she will be caught up in someone else's discourse, separated from herself and dependent. We see that Rose has accepted risk (thrashing around), thereby demonstrating faith (belief that she will swim). Her decision to love without her love being returned resembles an act in that what appears as a kind of masochistic pain actually enables a better understanding of her own desire and establishes a new freedom. As Žižek explains:

> . . . in a situation of the forced choice, the subject makes the "crazy," impossible choice of, in a way, *striking at*

himself, at what is most precious to himself. This act, far from amounting to a case of impotent aggressivity turned on oneself, rather changes the co-ordinates of the situation in which the subject finds himself: by cutting himself loose from the precious object through whose possession the enemy kept him in check, the subject gains the space of free action. Is not such a radical gesture of "striking at oneself" constitutive of subjectivity as such? (2000, 122–23, emphasis in original)

If we continue the drowning metaphor, then the lover functions as a kind of life preserver that has been removed (removed itself?), so that Rose is forced to either learn to swim or drown. She could search for another life preserver, but that would inhibit the movement toward radical autonomy that she desires. Grasping a new life preserver would mean giving way on her desire and repeating the symptom.

In her investigation of "love," Rose chooses to embrace loss, exemplifying a shift from the discourse of the hysteric to the discourse of the analyst:

Let me then be destroyed. For that is the only way I may have a chance of surviving. Let those feelings uniquely called forth by sexual love, my life's passion and pain, my learnt desirability figured out of my primeval undesirability, let them prevail. Now I am not dissociated from my ululation. I hear the roaring and the roasting and know that it is I. Resist the telephone! Even though help is only a few digits away. For the first time, I say "No" to any alleviation, to the mean of friendship, to the endlessly inventive love of my sisters. I don't want to be justified. Keep your mind in hell and . . . I want to sob and sob and sob . . . until the prolonged shrieking becomes a shout of joy.

"Loss" means that the original gift and salvation of love have been degraded: love's arrow poisoned and sent swiftly back into the heart. My time-worn remedy has been to pluck the arrow and to prove the wound, testing its resources with Protestant concentration. This time I want to do it differently. You may be weaker than the whole world, but you are always stronger than yourself. Let me send my power against my power. So what

if I die. Let me discover what it is that I want and fear
from love. Power and love, might and grace. That I may
desire again. I would be the Lover, am barely the Beloved.
(1995b, 74–75)

Her past strategy of plucking the arrow to "prove the wound" reflects
the hysteric's investigation of the signifier's lack. Such a strategy
stops at the recognition of her howling; it separates the wound from
the investigator. In wanting to do it differently, Rose moves to the
discourse of the analyst, first by insisting on physically experiencing
her desire and then by refusing to have her ego soothed in the usual
ways, such as comfort from her sisters, that would simply return her
to her previous self.

In claiming her own "roasting," Rose expresses a wish to get
beyond simple narcissistic desire (the imaginary) to an understanding
of a desire that was previously unconscious. When she says "that is
the only way I may have a chance of surviving," she implies that
through a recognition of this greater desire she may live in sym-
biosis with it and not be held captive by her symptoms. And she
expresses a readiness to take this step in such statements as "Let me
be destroyed" and "So what if I die." The relaxation of attachments
to Rose's ego allows the risk. Sending "my power against my power,"
the strength of the unconscious is recognized as greater than the
ego, and discovering what she wants and fears from love is a means
of accessing that power. By understanding her own desires around
love, Rose can become the lover and not be confined to the desire
of the other as represented by the beloved. The subjective destitution presented in this passage allows her to create an autonomous
subject for whom, not coincidentally, the trappings of the temporal
world hold little value.

And in doing it differently, we also see a different writing style.
The structure of grammar and syntax is relaxed as Rose takes greater
risks with her language. As she approaches her desire, she must find a
new way of expressing that search and discovery, and in the exchange
of power that makes language, she is able to discard the power of
the university discourse—academic language—as she accesses the
power of her own desire, which is best suited to the memoir form.
Fragments and ellipses may imply confusion, but they also imply
directness, a departure from the script, and hence a directness of
feeling. Her language and her focus on herself convey the effects of
this subjective destitution.

Love's Work

Rose's declaration and assumption of her own desire finishes Chapter 5 of *Love's Work*, but the power of language and symbols is evoked again at the beginning of Chapter 6:

> Suppose I were now to reveal that I have AIDS, full-blown AIDS, and have been ill during most of the course of what I have related. I would lose you. I would lose you to a knowledge, to a fear and to metaphor. Such a revelation would result in the sacrifice of the alchemy of my art, of artistic "control" over the setting as well as the content of your imagination. A double sacrifice of my elocution: to the unspeakable (death) and to the overspoken (AIDS).
>
> Not that I haven't been wooing you continually by the moods of metaphor; but we have kept the terms of our contract: you have given me free rein, and I have honoured my share of the obligation by not using up that freedom, by leaving large tracks of compacted equivocation at every twist of the telling.
>
> Yet, do you not know and fear even more about love? Yes, yes, of course you do, but while the sorrows of love in their monotony are endlessly engaging, illness is intrinsically not. So why should I deliberately spoil this narration by reduced equivocation? I must continue to write for the same reason I am always compelled to write, in sickness and in health: for, otherwise, I die deadly but this way, by this work, I may die forward into the intensified agon of living. (1995b, 76–77)

By presenting this information hypothetically, Rose is able to reflect on the relationship established by convention between the reader and writer of the memoir and to initiate the reevaluation of that contract. And by making her hypothetical illness AIDS instead of cancer, she exposes the power of the signifier before its connotations can take root. If, as Susan Sontag has asserted, "Societies need to have one illness which becomes identified with evil, and attaches blame to its 'victims' " (1990, 104), then AIDS has replaced cancer as that disease. Because AIDS represents more than just a physical illness, it is our best example of how the imaginary dictates the meaning and understanding of illness. Rose suspects (correctly, in my opinion) that she would lose the reader's trust if she now admitted to having had full-blown

AIDS while narrating the text up to that point, because in the public imagination, having AIDS would redefine every element of her life. Omitting that information breaks the unspoken agreement between reader and writer on which aspects of life are important or unimportant. And hiding such information would expose Rose's perspective as too unorthodox to be believable. But by invoking AIDS as a possibility, along with her power as author to shape the narrative, Rose forces readers to question their complicity in this narrative and to examine to what extent the subject that she presents is constructed to please the reader. Adopting the hysteric's discourse once again, she forces the reader to momentarily share the groundless ground she herself has adopted.

In Rose's text, discussing the specifics of cancer, similar to evoking AIDS, is equated with spoiling the narration. She discusses aspects of the body—shit, her colostomy—that disturb contemporary concepts of self by presenting pieces of the bodily real. At this point, her body becomes the stumbling block, that element that cannot be synthesized into her "self" through ordinary, approved discourse. In the same way that learning German provided Rose with a way to experience her dyslexia, writing the memoir and describing her colostomy connect her to her body, making that body a part of herself in a new way. And it is precisely Rose's claiming of her diseased body, as opposed to the strategies of peaceful detachment or military engagement against it, that turns this attitude into an act: "For what people seem to find most daunting with me, I discover, is not my illness or possible death, but my accentuated being; not my morbidity, but my renewed vitality" (1995b, 79). Rose accepts the lack or failure of her own body in the same way she accepts the failure of the love affair: it presents an opportunity for her to experience her own feelings and to incorporate the knowledge gained into a more complete, synthesized life. In refusing to place cancer in its usual taxonomies, Rose challenges the structures that replicate power, particularly the definition of the ill as Other that eases the minds of the healthy.[9]

By placing the story of her illness in the middle of *Love's Work*, Rose is able to situate her cancer in the context of a life philosophy—her "existential drama"—and thereby to evade the dominant tendency to interpret a life, like a story, solely through its ending. Just as she was not content to let Hume write her essay on Hume, even though it received praise, Rose refuses to let the discourses of cancer, the medical establishment, or New Age spirituality determine the narrative of her life. The comforts that the medical establishment and New Age spirituality might provide fail, in her mind, because they do not accommodate lack, and the work against lack is precisely what connects her to life. Rose describes medicine as a foreign language, one of which she knows words and phrases, "but never proceed[s] to grasp the underlying principles of grammar and syntax, which would give [her] the freedom to use the language creatively and critically" (102–103). The discourse of medicine is foreign to her because it follows the discourse of the university and the master, and therefore it does not connect to her desire. Rose wants to use it creatively, pursuing "alternative questions and conclusions," but this is the opposite goal of its advocates, who want to eliminate questions and institute order. For the doctors, the language of medicine is clear and unequivocal, whereas Rose discerns the gaps in what they say: "I perceive all the more pellucidly the subliminal beat: what you cannot cure, you condemn, so that you restore the equilibrium of your dangerous inner impulses" (103). Having embraced the danger of her impulses as a life philosophy, the equilibrium of the university discourse offers no satisfaction. Her cancer is, indeed, incurable, but Rose's reaction is to accept that cancer as something that supports and enables the challenges of love's work, which, by the end of the memoir, she reestablishes as a master discourse that does not alienate her from her body or from her desire.

Rose presents New Age spirituality as being just as closed and oppressive as medical discourse. It insists on an equilibrium that disallows the human; the authority of New Age, however, lies in the purity of the transcendent:

> It burdens the individual soul with an inner predestination: you have eternal life only if you dissolve the difficulty of living, of love of self and other, of the other in the self, if you are translucid, without inner or outer boundaries. If you lead a normally unhappy life, you are predestined to eternal damnation, you will not live.
>
> This is the counsel of despair which would keep the mind out of hell. The tradition is far kinder in its understanding that to live, to love, is to be failed, to forgive, to have failed, to be forgiven, for ever and ever. Keep your mind in hell and despair not. (1995b, 105)

This language without boundaries denies desire just as much as the language with too rigid boundaries. It proposes an ideal that cannot be achieved, and in turn it becomes oppressive for Rose. Rose's motto, "Keep your mind in hell, and despair not," taken from Staretz Silouan and used as an epigraph, exemplifies a paradox and complexity that, according to her, these other discourses do not allow. To keep one's mind in hell entails experiencing the position between two deaths. This position or perspective frees one from the confines of whole-ness and perfection and therefore enables the establishment of a new, more effective discourse.[10] Denial of this hellish situation would force Rose to continually work to maintain an illusion, while a relentless fight would likewise confine her to a life determined by her illness. By keeping her mind in hell, she has shifted to an infinite view that enables her to continue to experience her own desire.

Rose illustrates this paradox with the term *love's work*, a process of surrendering control that demands both risk and faith:

> "Control" in this context has two distinct meanings, both equally crucial. In the first place, "control," as you would expect, means priority and ability to manage, not to force, the compliance of others, to determine what others think or do. In the second, more elusive sense—a sense which, nevertheless, saves my life and which, once achieved, may induce the relinquishing of "control" in the first sense—"control" means that when something untoward happens, some trauma or damage, whether inflicted by the commis-sions or omissions of others, or some cosmic force, one makes the initially unwelcome event one's own inner occupation. You work to adopt the most loveless, forlorn, aggressive child as your own, and do not leave her to develop into an even more vengeful monster, who constantly wishes you ill. In ill health as in unhappy love, this is the hardest work: it requires taking in before letting be. (1995b, 97–98)

The second definition of control presented demands as its first step an acceptance, and the examples of unhappy love and ill health reflect the traumas of desire and fate, respectively. Rose has gained control by developing a new master signifier, "love's work," which as a process allows for continuous displacement and change. As such, love's work provides a way of gaining knowledge without institutionalizing that knowledge as a new university or master discourse. Instead of banish-ing what is other, Rose makes the difficult demand to love what is killing her, which illustrates the identification with the symptom that signals the end of analysis for Lacan. In her adoption of the aggres-sive child (an allusion to herself?), she has moved from symptom to *sinthome*. The abstractness and equivocation demanded by "love's work," or the metaphor of the aggressive child, will allow Rose to be unequivocal when it comes to topics such as her colostomy; she embraces what is typically repressed, claiming her symptom as her own as is possible within a philosophy of love's work but not within a philosophy of propriety or formal knowledge. And Rose regains her readers' trust precisely through her specificity, which reveals a willingness to discard the dominant discourse both in what she says and how she says it. In prioritizing her symptom, Rose moves to the genre of memoir—the sloppy, vulgar, and undisciplined sibling of philosophy and the novel.

The Products of Love's Work

Thus we see that in *Love's Work* the four discourses come full circle. Lacan explains, however, that because the subject produces the new master signifiers herself—because she tells her own story—the signifiers and the subject's desire come closer together, and the alienating power of the master's discourse is diminished. Summarizing Lacan, Bracher states that the discourse of the analyst allows the subject to "assume its own alienation and desire and, on the basis of that assumption, separate from the given master signifiers and produce its own new master signifiers, that is, ideals and values less inimical to its fundamental fantasy and the desire embodied by that fantasy" (1993, 68). We see this cycle continue in *Paradiso*, as the master signifier of "love's work" is replaced once again. In *Paradiso*, Rose searches for a language of praise to replace the agonistic strategy of love's work.

Rose's first portrait in *Paradiso* is of her friend, Sister Edna, and Rose explains, "It was the desire to communicate [Sister Edna's] radiant goodness that gave birth to this whole work in which I am engaged" (1999, 15). Rose's connection to Edna's goodness, however, developed out of her own need when faced with unfamiliar feelings of contentment. Habituated to interrogating the Other—writing the discourse of the hysteric—Rose finds she has no method with which to praise:

> And I turn to Edna for help: I need help in my state of bliss. For I am well practised in the arts of resignation and in the prayer that they provoke. O God, take away this pain, this punishment—prayer in adversity. Yet I have no liturgy for thanksgiving, for praise, for consummation;

for my well-being, love-ability, or for a new sensation; a constant awareness of existence, alone or in the company of others, imbued with a silly palpability, a beauty at once tactile and visual—as if on each intake of breath one were immersing one's hands in the deep folds of some fine material saturated in glorious colour. How to give this beauty back? I ask Edna if I can see her in order to try and speak to her about my condition of doxological terror. The withdrawal of the abyss, the overwhelming plenitude of every moment, leaves me more vulnerable than the busy tumult of distress: I have nothing to clutch, nothing to point to as my burden, nothing from which to bet alleviation. My soul is naked: it has lost its scaffolding of regret and remorse or even repentance: it is turned: and the unexpected result is the sensation and the envelope of invisible and visible beauty. (1999, 20–21)

Having dropped the scaffolding of the agonistic ego, Rose is overwhelmed by the fullness of beauty and of existence. Moving further into separation, she loses the moorings of alienation, and she turns to Edna for a new, "less inimical" language to describe her experience. Not having learned the language of gratitude or praise at university, Rose turns to her religious friend, still wary and frightened by authority, for a discourse of the church.

As the traditions of nation and church have shown, however, praise is also intimately linked to power and authority. How can Rose convey her own bliss or Edna's goodness without imposing her or Edna's method as law? Rose's solution lies, somewhat surprisingly, in the figure of Miss Marple (who shares Edna's advanced age). According to Rose, Marple has given up ego attachments and focuses on observing the world around her. Her interest is not in how she is seen and desired by the other but to "be in the image of another Truth and to receive it and grow into it" (1999, 18). And faith enters this equation through the belief that if desire coincides with something higher, it will not oppress but instead improve the greater world. Stripped of symbolic roots (How does she appear in these different places? Doesn't she have her own responsibilities?), she appears as a pure receptacle for knowledge.

Rose then goes on to describe her own practice of praise. Suffering from feelings of nausea and disorientation while riding a train, she uses the image of Edna not as model but as prayer:

Think of Sister Edna.
Think of sister Edna.
Think of sister Edna.
Think of sister Edna.
The beat of the train takes up your name. (1999, 22)

In a somewhat mystical fashion, the inner thought of Edna merges with the outside rhythm of the train. Internal and external worlds harmonize. Through the prayer, Edna's goodness affects Rose, her nausea abates, and from this experience Rose imagines her next project:

> Gradually, as I sit bolt upright, the nausea abates, and this work comes to me. I will write a Paradiso which will be a series of descants on friends and family who have somehow passed beyond purgatory, who have dwelt in the abyss, in hell, and undergone purgation. I will write about goodness and its fruits: under the names of Edna and Hariklia. (1999, 22–23)

In this example, Rose chooses not to focus on her own physical pain but replaces it with the greater goodness of Edna. The leap of faith exemplified in the detachment from one's self is rewarded with the solution to the problem: a discourse for her gratitude. Metaphorically, both love and illness have been Rose's own hell and purgation, the nausea standing in primarily for her experience with cancer and secondarily for the roasting she experienced in disappointed love. In this example, as in the analyst's discourse, knowledge is produced by placing it in the position of product, not as agent or other. Rose's desire, stemming from her discomfort, addresses Edna as incomplete subject, and the product is an understanding of goodness (S1) that she is able to put into discourse (S2). Paradise, then, is the integration of desire and knowledge into a transmissible form, and the analyst's discourse is less likely to become authoritarian because of the temporal and unique nature of desire and the lacking subject. As Rose separates even farther from the mundane world, we see that she establishes yet again a new master discourse, the discourse of praise, that accommodates her failing body and her limited ability to work. While the discourse of the hysteric, so prominent in *Love's Work*, allowed Rose to see lack and therefore work continuously to fill that lack, the master discourse she establishes in *Paradiso* facilitates the reception of beauty and goodness. As Fink explains, "Every discourse requires a loss of jouissance and has its own mainspring or truth" (1995, 137). This is particularly evident in the shift between these two autobiographical texts, as the pleasure of protest is exchanged for the pleasure of praise.

Writing on the popularity of the confession in modern discourse, Dennis Foster asserts:

> We have lost the Author, the master of meanings, intentions, and language. But we have something more interesting, even if more insidious: a master who doesn't know, a leader with no course. The writer in this view has no truth, but has a language that has developed out of the labor and accidents of life, something peculiar to him, his to use but not fully to control: a discourse. (1997, 4)

What Foster presents here, and what many writers on postmodernism have claimed, is that the kind of writing characterized as the discourse of the university—codified knowledge—has lost its efficacy. We no longer have the Author with a capital "A." In this age of skepticism, rigid authority has lost its aura and its ability to capture our desire. And yet this knowledge that the big Other no longer exists does not necessarily create joyous freedom. One could argue that smaller authorities have proliferated as we look for guides and experts for even more specific elements of our lives. The modern memoir, I would argue, participates in this movement and reflects the popular value placed not in codified regimes of knowledge but in the belief that self-knowledge is most likely to lead to contentment. Therefore, although memoirs are still written by political figures, military heroes, and intellectuals who gain their authority from their place in the symbolic order, the proliferation of memoirs by people who have made no other dominant mark on society reflects this belief that a narrative of self-knowledge has value and deserves a public audience. *Love's Work* is typical of this type of modern memoir in that its use and movement through the four discourses present a paradigm for altering one's discursive position. While ostensibly presenting a form of self-knowledge, the success of Rose's autobiographical writing lies in her ability to convey that the pursuit of self-knowledge is bound to fail, and her ability to clothe that failure in a sublime beauty.

The memoir is a paradox in that on one level it presents a one-to-one correspondence. The autobiographer takes herself as the protagonist and, conventionally, these two identities coincide. However, what drives the narrative of a memoir is precisely the noncoincidence of the author and the narrator. That gap is what the memoirist attempts to fill. We see in Rose's work, particular the shift from *Love's Work* to

Paradiso, that this gap is never filled once and for all. The separate peace made by the author of the memoir functions similarly to the marriage that often ends the novel. It is an artificial closure that suggests a sequel to evaluate the newly established master signifiers such as "marriage" and "love's work."

To change one's fundamental fantasy may, in fact, be more heroic than a stubborn commitment to ideals in the face of death. In writing a memoir, one gives oneself over to language and risks not liking what appears on the page. Knowledge may be gained that proves one's structuring principles to be false. The attractiveness of the memoir, however, is the bridge it presents between writing and life. As in the stories told by Walter Benjamin's artisans, it conveys wisdom, not information.[11] Rose expresses a similar idea: "However satisfying writing is—that mix of discipline and miracle, which leaves you in control, even when what appears on the page has emerged from regions beyond your control—it is a very poor substitute indeed for the joy and the agony of loving" (1995b, 59). In the memoir, writing is not love, but in allowing love to be defined by the "regions beyond your control," the memoirist illustrates how the self is never stable, how it (and therefore the ways that we love) is continuously altered by the symbolic (discipline) and the real (miracle). The best memoirs do not give advice. They illustrate how experiences such as love, writing, and death are determined by particular discourses. And in illustrating these different discourses, they convey to the reader choice, freedom, and possibility.

CHAPTER 4

Harold Brodkey's Traversal of Fiction

This Wild Darkness *as* La Passe

The time is out of joint: O cursed spite,
That ever I was born to set it right!

—*Hamlet*, Shakespeare

American author Harold Brodkey was famous for his mystifications. Although he wrote primarily fiction until the end of his life, all of his work contained autobiographical elements, thus inviting speculation as to the extent to which life and fiction overlapped. In addition, Brodkey established a reputation as a man about town in New York. Dalliances with both men and women mystified his sexual and romantic life and ensured that he would be discussed. His publishing and writing habits also invited speculation, as rumors of a magnum opus were frequently spread and publication dates announced without the book appearing. People suspected that Brodkey, like J. D. Salinger, had multiple manuscripts locked away in a closet.[1] Brodkey viewed ultimate truth as unattainable; therefore, he created multiple fictions, or alternative truths. In his fictional work, Brodkey changed reality through doubles, alter egos, and fictions that in turn reinforced the inferiority of commonly perceived "reality."

The result was a fictional style that could be either transcendent or meaningless, depending on the mood and patience of the reader. Brodkey's fiction relentlessly examines every thought and change of light, drawing few conclusions, all in the attempt to stop time and establish moments of "being" that are fleeting and elusive. Near the end of his life, however, Brodkey changes his style. Of course the primary shift is from fiction to autobiography, but in addition, his style becomes clearer and more direct. Presented with an AIDS diagnosis and only a few years to live,[2] Brodkey explains (significantly, in letter form, "to his readers") the mystifications throughout his work and begins to shut down the imaginative matrix that constitutes his fiction.[3] Instead of provoking a fear of death, Brodkey's diagnosis actually frees him from a dominating attachment to a lost wholeness manifested in his fiction and also frees him from the responsibility of maintaining the status of that fictional world. Indeed, he finds that terminal illness provides relief: "It was a relief to have the illness unmasked, to have Death be openly present. It was a relief to get away from the tease and rank of imputed greatness and from the denial and attacks and from my own sense of things, of worldly reality and of literary reality—all of it. . . . It was a relief to have the future not be my speculative responsibility anymore and to escape from games of superiority and inferiority" (1994, 74). We see that terminal illness frees Brodkey from the demands of finite games, from the competition for prizes and titles. The change in tone from Brodkey's fiction to his memoir suggests that an awareness of mortality has vitiated the power of his familiar way of seeing and describing the world, a habit that seemed protective but that was, in fact, deadening.

In this chapter I examine changes in style from Brodkey's fiction to his memoir and the effect of his 1993 AIDS diagnosis on the form and content of that memoir. Specifically, I suggest that Brodkey's memoir reflects a process similar to the psychoanalytic Pass (*la Passe*) developed in the 1960s by Jacques Lacan. The Pass is a process within the training analysis that verifies the analysand's movement to the position of analyst. To complete the Pass, the *passant* tells the story of his or her analysis to two randomly selected people, who then convey the case to a deciding panel. This unusual insertion of a mediator between the judging body and the person being judged reveals Lacan's concern that the analyst surrender authority and be able to speak from a place without ego, or from the position of the dead. Accepting this powerlessness testifies to the analysand's rearrangement or "traversing" of his most basic fantasy.[4] Brodkey's memoir and, one could argue, the memoir in general, resembles this surrendering process as he narrates his story to a group of readers who are mostly strangers. Indeed, Brodkey's text reveals that the memoir, like the Pass, not only announces but also *enacts* the separation from a particular fantasy, and therefore both are necessary steps in establishing a new fantasy that is more compatible with the subject's altered position in the world.

Integration and the Literary Memoir

In *Theory of the Novel*, Georg Lukacs (1971) attempts to connect the development of a genre to historical conditions, tracing the rise of the novel and contrasting it with the epic. For Lukacs, the novel is an inherently melancholy form. It reveals a separation between "the conventionality of the objective world and the interiority of the subjective one" (70). The driving force of the novel is the attempt to breach this separation, and through that reconnection to discover a meaning for life. Because no ultimate meaning can be found, however, the search then becomes the novel's true subject matter, and because of the absence of ultimate meaning, Lukacs defines the novel as "the epic of a world that has been abandoned by God." The novel conveys "that meaning can never quite penetrate reality, but that, without meaning, reality would disintegrate into the nothingness of inessentiality" (88). Because we do not live in an "integrated civilisation," and because we have no clear meaning for human experience, the novelist seeks to provide meaning by creating an imagined world. The inability to create a complete world is the source of fiction's melancholia, but its compensation is the pleasure of the search.

Lukacs derives his conclusions from a contrast between the epic, that product of an integrated civilization, and the novel, the product of a "problematic" civilization. Walter Benjamin, in his 1968 essay "The Storyteller: Reflections on the Works of Nikolai Leskov," builds on Lukacs's premise and applies similar criteria to the genre of the story, particularly the orated story. Benjamin describes the categories of integrated and problematic civilizations in terms of communicable experience. He compares the largely superseded genre of storytelling, where the author conveys counsel and in which the reader invests meaning, to information, which has only momentary value and hence no noticeable effect on the recipient's life. Storytelling, like Lukacs's epic, weaves counsel "into the fabric of real life," creating what Benjamin calls "wisdom." Both epic and storytelling suggest a community in which meanings are shared and developed through exchange. The novel and information, to different degrees, both convey the isolation of experience and the transience of meaning. Thus in both Lukacs's and Benjamin's analysis of these linguistic forms, the structure and function of the genre is tied to the demands and abilities of the community. The popularity, and even existence, of a particular genre depends on what the community accepts as true and what readers believe they can use. When the meaning of events is not certain and differences in background preclude the sharing of experiences, new genres are developed to accommodate that confusion.

I use Lukacs's and Benjamin's texts to explore some other elements that define the memoir as a genre. The immediate criterion that separates the memoir from its structural sibling, the novel, is that it is supposedly true.[5] The label "memoir" suggests that the events narrated actually happened. Any marginally sophisticated reader doubts this claim of truth, however. The reader will probably accept that the author believes these events to have happened, or perhaps, even more skeptically, that the author simply wants us to believe that the events actually occurred. This combination of belief and skepticism is still markedly different from our belief and skepticism toward fiction. In fiction, we are asked to accept that the narrative has sprung from the author's imagination, and that the events did *not* happen. Instead of doubting the author's objectivity, we often doubt the power of the author's imagination and assume that the work of fiction is a modified translation of actual events. However similar the novel and memoir appear on the surface, the premise from which we begin reading the texts is radically different based on this distinction. The simple inclusion of "a memoir" or "a novel" on the cover shapes how we read and understand the words. Is the author working with events and situations beyond her control? How much of the narrative is subject to her will? I suggest that the lack of control that is central to the memoir as a genre separates it even farther from epic truth, that is, from a truth that is universal and transparent. Indeed, precisely that lack of control makes the genre appealing to a culture searching for relevance, or "the fabric of real life."

Brodkey discusses the role of fiction in several essays collected in the 1999 volume *Sea Battles on Dry Land*. For Brodkey, fiction provides a different kind of wisdom. It does not describe how things are, but how they could be. In these essays, particularly 1994's "Fiction Is Fictional," Brodkey views the communicability of experience in a similar way to Lukacs and Benjamin, categorizing elements through the same binary of realism versus idealism. Brodkey is equally fearful of the proliferation of useless images that Benjamin labeled "information," images that he sees predominantly in advertising. For Brodkey, culture determines how information and ideas are conveyed, and therefore controls the stories that are told:

Culture, the ways we have been educated, and individual taste helps us decide what is worth knowing in stories—this is where form gets mixed with content. Our culture—the modern, technological, media-centered one—tries for a retelling that covers everything really, but we have no time for that, for everything. So stories, even in movies, deal in representative moments. Those moments represent everything the way Congress is supposed to represent all of us (ha-ha). (1999, 351)

According to Brodkey, the culture that established modern prose fiction is an oversimplifying, teleological, capitalist culture that has appropriated transcendence, or, in Benjamin's terms, has denied eternity and death. Brodkey believes that "Capitalism presents a one-tier, pretty-much-omnipotence-and-omniscience-ruled world with the claim that people, women and men, share in that omnipotence-and omniscience" (1999, 353). The consequence of this subjugation of omnipotence and omniscience is constant disappointment and despair, because our actual lives never fulfill this promise. And, like Lukacs, he believes as a consequence we create a lost utopia out of our youth.

Brodkey thus shares the melancholy of Lukacs and Benjamin towards modern life, but for him prose fiction serves as a comfort for this disappointment, not as a further reflection of the distance culture has traveled from epic integration and meaningful life. Fiction, for Brodkey, is a "pragmatic transcendence," in which the ability to see and remember is improved by the imagination, thus making life more bearable. One can transcend the mundane through thought and will. The distance between fiction and life that defined fiction's uselessness for Benjamin is precisely what makes it valuable for Brodkey. Fiction is not constrained by what really happened:

The unreality of prose fiction, the lie, means it cannot be photographed or filmed, although ideas for visible stories can be drawn from it. And at the same time, no evidence from the past can prove or disprove the story, the fiction, or add to it factually: the damn thing was never true in that sense. It was, or is, true (or not) in another sense, but this other sense is grander and has to do with final meaning, laws of behavior and theories about them worked out as destiny in the story, moral or amoral principles both personal and of the universe. (1999, 354)

Thus, for Brodkey, fiction serves universal truths but is not valuable in a practical way. Brodkey repeatedly groups fiction with the "lie," as well as "charm, gestures, and art," and contrasts these with the limits of a utilitarian reality.

What is striking about his insistence on the "unreality" of fiction is the similarity between the events Brodkey describes in his fiction and the events of his own life. Wiley Silenowicz, the narrator of many of Brodkey's stories and of his novel *The Runaway Soul*, is orphaned as a child, adopted by close relatives who already have a daughter, attends Harvard, and confronts the early deaths of his adoptive parents just as the real Harold Brodkey did. As Brodkey insists in his article "Fiction Is Fictional," prose fiction explores the unreal and unseeable aspects of the past: using memory to reconfigure the past by temporarily inhabiting that imaginative space (1999, 355). As a result, most of Brodkey's fiction could be described as conversations with the dead. He uses memory to create a world in which the dead still exist, and he imagines how he was seen by them and what kind of happiness he provided. The fiction thus becomes a means of continuing these relationships beyond the grave in order to [re]experience the pleasure and knowledge they provided.

The real world of dates and commitments, therefore, conflicts with Brodkey's fictional world, and he must be protected from it:

> It is less odd to watch a story being enacted than to hear one extemporized, and to hear one is less odd than to read one, although we may prefer to read in order to escape the presence of other people. Among people, we live among actual stories. We do that diagnostically; we watch each other, watch things happen, nosily or out of caution or in sympathy or by necessity in real life. We have to figure them out, have to make stories of events. It is a privilege to ignore people and events—if you're not punished for it. (1999, 351)

In this passage Brodkey contrasts the way he makes stories with the way people construct narratives in everyday life. The normal, or "less odd," story is one of action. And when he suggests that to hear a story is less odd than to read one, he reinforces Benjamin's idea that the orated story is more connected to life. We read, however, to "escape the presence of other people," and since other people "live among actual stories," Brodkey defines actual stories as a dangerous enterprise. Brodkey, being privileged enough to ignore many things,

reshapes events by writing fiction, and therefore writing is by definition connected to the unreal, or more accurately, the imaginary. The
privilege is being able to write his own story instead of participating
in culturally dictated plots.

"Fiction Is Fictional" helped me understand an anecdote I read
about Brodkey several years ago. Writing in *The Nation*, J. D. Dolan
(1996) describes his last meeting with Brodkey while he was tending
a bar inhabited by only one other patron:

> The other man at the bar became interested.
> He said to Harold, "Are you a writer?"
> Harold looked at his brandy and said, "Yes, I'm a writer."
> "Really?" the man said. "I love to read. What's your
>   name?"
> "What do you read?" Harold said.
> "Well, I like to read a lot of stuff," the man said.
> Harold waited.
> "Well, I like John le Carre," the man said.
> "Middlebrow," Harold said. "But I have the same editor
>   as le Carre, the same agent."
> "What?" the man said, and I saw in his expression a flicker
>   of panic. Then the man recovered and said, "You do?
>   What's your name?"
> Harold stared at his brandy.
> "I read *The New Yorker*," the man added.
> "Hmm," Harold said. "I write for *The New Yorker*."
> "Really, what's your name?"
> Harold finished his brandy and said, "It's getting late."
> "Wait a minute, what's your name?" the man asked. "I'd
>   like to read something of yours."
> Harold finally looked at the man and said, "I realize that
>   you have no way of knowing who I am. I understand
>   that. I just feel that you should already know who I
>   am. I know it's absurd." (1996, 35–36)

Brodkey's behavior in this scene appears rude and egomaniacal, but
his recognition of the absurdity of his behavior complicates the situation. In this example, Brodkey asserts his privilege to "ignore people
and events"; in order to believe the myth of his own reputation he
must ignore actual experience, here the questions and knowledge (or
lack of knowledge) of the stranger. And in this situation Dolan fails
to protect him, both from the stranger and, by publishing the story,

from the public at large. The event provides a story for Dolan and for me, in that we choose to turn it into a "representative moment."

Brodkey believes, however, that the role of fiction is to avoid such simple readings of actual events. The freed mind escapes doctrine (the need to answer direct questions, such as "What is your name?") and makes alternative worlds available:

> The point here perhaps is that many aspects of our species are invisible in the way a prose fiction is—thought, dream, memory, feelings, acts of thought, a dream episode, acts of memory. The portrayal of things unseen (and unseeable) is sort of the heart of the whole project. Invisible activities of the mind seem to be the models for fictions or, if you like, unphysical, unbodied tales. A tentative conclusion would be that only a mind cut off from the world and escaped from doctrine (a discipline for the mind) and rebellious toward it can make fiction, can narrate a prose fiction. Thought, dream, and memory become experientially available (to study, to look at, to draw on) only in states and fairly long-term situations of mental freedom. In unfree situations, those acts of consciousness as models are constrained by revelation, by decree. (1999, 355)

In the bar scene described by Dolan, the stranger determines that Brodkey's place in the symbolic order is insignificant even though at the same time he shows a willingness to revise this opinion and an implicit respect for all "writers." But it is precisely the man's power over Brodkey's identity that makes the bar an "unfree situation." The anecdote illustrates how Brodkey's theories of fiction carry over into his life.

Brodkey's statement, that the fiction writer must cut himself off from the world, reveals both his similarity and difference from the Lukacs of *Theory of the Novel*. Lukacs states in his 1962 preface that "the problems of the novel form are here [in this book] the mirror image of a world out of joint," and that "reality no longer constitutes a favourable soil for art" (1971, 17). Brodkey also sees the world as being out of joint, but fiction becomes an antidote to the imperfect world. As a fiction writer, Brodkey believes his work can make the world a better place by changing the way people see: "I am trying to change consciousness, change language in such a way that the modes of behavior I am opposed to become unpopular, absurd, unlikely. You try to work toward a culture that takes time and conscience seriously in a real way and not as part of a tidal flow of hype" (Linville 1991, 90). Lukacs's utopian perspective suggests that a better world would produce better art forms. Brodkey believes that good art (his art) can produce a better world.

Of course, the implicit judgment in Brodkey's comments is that "modern" fiction, the kind of fiction he admires and writes, is abstract. "Fiction, modern fiction, is a form of story in which the mind is prevented from moving toward a hazy total" (1999, 351). This fiction is imagistic, disconnected, and self-conscious; it is not the realistic novel of the nineteenth century, or the novels of his *bete noire*, John Updike. But what happens when he is unable to keep the events of the world at bay? When he cannot simply walk out of the bar and dismiss the Other? And how does the "Brodkey method" apply to a genre such as the memoir, which is supposedly based on what really happened?

The Desire of the Other

To avoid turning life into a series of oversimplified representative moments, Brodkey focuses his attention on the unspoken and the implied within human interactions. He is particularly interested in how we interpret the desires of others and how those interpretations shape behavior. Indeed, one could argue that the dominant theme of Brodkey's fiction is his position as object of desire within this secondary world of memory and imagination.

In *This Wild Darkness*, Brodkey (1996) narrates the facts of this objectification and how they reflect what he calls his "irresistibility," a quality that, in his narration, caused traumatic events and determined his life.[6] Brodkey explains that he has always experienced demands from others that he could not satisfy: "From infancy, my life has always been, always, always, on the verge of my being eaten alive: *I could just eat you up.* In my childhood, people talked a great deal about me and quarreled over me—and threatened force" (1996, 54, emphasis in original). Brodkey is the object from which others derive pleasure, and this position as object clearly presents an obstacle to his attempts to establish his own subjectivity. He perceives making others happy as his duty, and this is most clearly seen in his perception that his affection for his parents kept them alive. The role as object of desire—represented by his irresistibility—continues into adulthood, but Brodkey explains that he learned to avoid and control these attentions through a brusque and self-centered demeanor that, one could argue, actually intensified his mysteriousness and allure.

While Brodkey is able, with effort, to deflect many of his suitors and critics in his adult life, he is able to engage fully with that attention in his fiction. In "A Story in an Almost Classical Mode," the narrator explains his relationship with his dying mother and her dependence on him: "All right, her happiness rested on me. Her sister and one brother and her daughter told me I couldn't go to college, I couldn't leave Doris, it would be a crime" (1989, 258). Similarly, in "His Son, in His Arms, in Light, Aloft" the father's moods and feelings are determined by the son:

> ... he lays his sensibility aside or models his on mine, on my joy, takes his emotional coloring from me, like a mirror or a twin: his incomprehensible life, with its strength, ordeals, triumphs, crimes, horrors, his sadness and disgust, is enveloped and momentarily assuaged by my direct and indirect childish consolation. (1989, 279)

We see in these examples from the stories that Brodkey is able to imagine existence before the primary trauma of his life: the loss of his parents. He repeatedly plays the game of *Che Vuoi?* (as elaborated by Lacan and Žižek) with his memories of his parents: What do they want from me? Who do they want me to be? The stories present a variety of answers to those questions, allowing Brodkey to remain connected to the dead and, more importantly, allowing him to repay his debt to the dead by proxy; his alter egos—Wiley Silenowicz and others—can turn themselves into objects of desire and restore the unity that Brodkey lost when he left his parents and became an orphan, two experiences that are connected in his imagination and fuel his suspicion that he is responsible for his parents' deaths.[7]

The picture Brodkey provides of life in his stories and before his AIDS diagnosis is of a person attached to the knowledge of suffering he learned from these traumatic experiences with his parents: "And, you see, a traumatized child, as I was once, long ago, and one who recovers, as I did, has a wall between him and pain and despair, between him and grief, between himself and beshitting himself" (1996, 9).[8] Brodkey's status as orphan defines him and establishes his outlook on the world. We see, however, that he has turned this loss, and the resulting "wall," into a marker of strength, wisdom, and uniqueness that provides satisfaction. The paradoxical combination of traumatic loss and pleasurable attachment to that loss is a familiar paradigm, as Bruce Fink explains:

> Castration is, after all, the imposition of a loss of satisfaction (for example, for a boy at the end of the Oedipal conflict, the loss of his mother or mother substitute as a primary libidinal object). That loss is forever regretted by the neurotic, the subject being unable to focus on the remaining possibilities of satisfaction. Instead, he or she "loves" his or her castration, obstinately clinging to that loss, refusing to find satisfaction elsewhere. (Fink 1997, 277)

In Brodkey's fiction we see the regret that he experiences toward his parents; the constant reconfiguring of those relationships becomes his primary libidinal object. Consequently, the immediate present becomes an intrusion, which is why Brodkey feels persecuted and why he continually looks for protection from the demands of others, primarily through the demands of his work.

This love of what he has lost helps explain Brodkey's relationship with his fictional alter ego, Wiley Silenowicz. In psychoanalytic terms, Silenowicz presents enjoyment structured by the discourse of the hysteric. Silenowicz, like the child-Brodkey, is dominated by the question that defines the hysteric: "What for an object am I in the eyes of the Other, for the Other's desire)?" (Žižek 1997, 117). This position reflects Brodkey's experience of being an object that was exchanged and manipulated at the whim of others, a position that he repudiated as an adult. However, he is able to maintain this particular pleasure by experiencing it indirectly through Silenowicz, which in turn demands the constant creation and maintenance of this alter ego, resulting in a frenetic overactivity that shuts out much of the world around him. This hyperactivity moves Brodkey himself closer to an obsessional structure, something that appears in his procrastination and constant reworking of what would become *The Runaway Soul*.[9] One can speculate that Brodkey was so fascinated by the experiences he could create for Silenowicz that publishing (like death) would demand a conclusion and a commitment to one narrative and hence an end to his enjoyment.

In *The Plague of Fantasies* Slavoj Žižek (1997) uses the concept of interpassivity to illustrate how these two structures—hysteric and obsessive—complement each other. Žižek explains "interpassivity" as being "passive through the other" (115): the subject accedes the passive activity of enjoying to the other, which allows him or her to remain constantly, often frenetically, active. The object is passive, which allows the subject to obsess on the object, separating him from his own enjoyment (116).[10] This dynamic of active work and passive enjoyment is precisely what we see between Brodkey and his literary alter ego, Wiley Silenowicz, who enjoys the attentions of Brodkey's dead relatives in Brodkey's place. In his fiction, Brodkey is able to explore how and why this alter ego responds to the love of others and thus what kind of object he is for these characters from memory. This creative effort displaces onto Silenowicz the anxiety Brodkey experiences when he is placed in the position of an object. This displacement allows him to choose his own object of desire which, interestingly, becomes the maintenance of the imaginative world that Silenowicz inhabits. Brodkey's fiction, like the bobbin and string in Freud's fort-da example, covers over a lack, enabling him to enjoy the disruptions of absence and presence, love and demand, in a controlled but not completely predictable way.

One way of viewing the memoir in Brodkey's *oeuvre* is as an exemplification of Freud's expression, "*Wo Es war, soll Ich werden*," which Lacan frequently discusses.[11] A fairly literal translation of the phrase is "Where it was, I shall become." In this expression, *Es* represents the real, which Fredric Jameson defines as "History itself" (1988, 104) or the course of events in Brodkey's life. *Ich*, in this case, is the subject coming into being through the writing of the memoir. The writing of the memoir reenacts the emergence of the subject through metaphoric substitution; in *This Wild Darkness* the *Ich* temporarily stands in for the *Es*; Brodkey's story, as he claims it, takes priority over the voices of his imagination and the oddities of fate. Therefore, his memoir has a much more practical and temporal effect than his fiction. It does not produce revelation, but reconciliation.

In *This Wild Darkness* Brodkey tells parts of the stories that established his mythology. He explains his adoption, the deaths of his parents, the sexual abuse by his father, his explorations of homosexuality, and the myth of his irresistibility. The difficulty that Brodkey has telling these stories honestly appears in his language:

> Anyway, the major drama of my adolescence was that my adoptive father, Joe Brodkey, who was ill with heart trouble (a handsome invalid, as one would write in pornography), assailed me every day for two years, sexually—twice a day, every morning and every evening, when I was twelve and thirteen. He had nothing else to do, really. He was ill. We were not the same blood. I am being very shy. He never succeeded in entering me, but it was somewhat scary and sweaty. Except that there was the pathos of his dying. And

there was my long history of boring irresistibility. And my mind, which was watching all of it. His blood pressure was fragilely high. I was too strong, too frozen, for very much to happen, for the drama to develop. I am lying. I had to notice that he was heartsick—with feeling, clearly in *love*, in a way. And soon, somehow, when I didn't make a scene about the assaults, or whatever, a great many people knew about "the love story." (1996, 58, emphasis in original)

Brodkey's absence in this excerpt is striking. Joe Brodkey, the "assailant," is described repeatedly, as his "adoptive father," "a handsome invalid" as having "nothing else to do," "fragilely high" blood pressure, and as "heartsick" and "in love." What we learn about Brodkey is his distance from the scene, his mind detached from his body, "watching all of it." He portrays his relationship with his father as a "love story" in which he is not a willing participant.

Brodkey does emerge in the commentary, however. "I am being very shy" and "I am lying" are perhaps the most revealing sentences of the passage, in that they express Brodkey's ambivalence. By using "I am lying," he tells the story two ways. First, as the frozen and unwilling adolescent, perhaps as Brodkey would like to appear. Then, as the young man who understands his father's desire and wants to please him. By exposing his own lie, Brodkey is able to show his knowledge of how he ought to feel alongside the feelings that make him uncomfortable. The agonizing conflict of parental abuse becomes strikingly clear as Brodkey attempts to fulfill his father's desire but tries not to fulfill this particular desire: "It is your own moral judgment that arranges this refusal of your father even though he is dying. Such refusal is arrogant toward Daddy. Or at least it places a positive value on your own life" (1996, 61).

Brodkey's denial of his father's demands circulates throughout his fiction as a lost moment of unity, and the stories illustrate the attempts of the guilt-ridden son to repay the ghost of his father. At the same time, the conflict with his father appears in the memoir as a determining factor of his life, directly linked to his disease: "He accursed me. Now I will die disfigured and in pain" (61). Brodkey connects his experimentation with homosexuality to his search for the truth of his relationship with his father. In Brodkey's mind, his father became metonymically connected to all men, and his relationships with men served as an exploration and a reenactment of his relationship with his father. Thus in his fiction Brodkey can create a transcendent, nonsexual unity with his father, but in the memoir, the ambivalence and conflict of actual circumstances force him into a simplistic conclusion, exactly what he believes fiction should avoid.

As he continues to explain the "love story," Brodkey places it in the context of his own "irresistibility," thereby taking responsibility for the actions of others and solidifying his identity as an object of desire. He explains that his affair with his father "helped keep both her [his mother] and Dad alive: it interested them, this love thing" (59), and that the desire of others for him could be equated with possession of him: "Whatever I was, it was not taken to be a private property and mine. I understood my father's actions on this level, in this light" (60). The need displayed by Brodkey's parents places him in a dyadic relation to both. He believes he completes them. And although this unity deprives him of a complete sense of self, it also provides him with momentary pleasure: "Such assaults as Joe's have their aspect of wanting to lower you, but at moments everything was focused, as if in the last line of a story, on a profound concern having to do with the creature in whom my identity was at the moment caught. Either of my parents would have killed the other for me" (59). In this passage Brodkey equates the melding of identities with the short story form. In "Fiction Is Fictional" he describes the story as "A life's moment, everything mad with significance as in poetry and dreams and music" (1999, 359). Like the affair, the story creates a focus that transcends time, the isolated ego, and therefore death. Traditional boundaries are violated, and the child-Brodkey acquires a value beyond life itself. Not only does he believe that his parents would kill for him, he believes he can keep them alive. The drawback, however, is that his value depends on their desire for him. Therefore, when Brodkey's parents die, he is left feeling responsible for those deaths and cut off from real happiness. The closest he can get to this ideal happiness is to maintain his parents in his own ego. Through memory and fiction, ideal unity remains possible and, even better, under Brodkey's control. Thus in Brodkey's narrative, to be "orphaned" takes on a metaphorical significance. It implies the loss of a complete wholeness and a separation from ordinary ideas of comfort.

Brodkey finishes his discussion of the "love story" with yet another connection between experience and writing style: "To tell a little of the story about me and my father less shyly, I would have to change the way I write. In real life, I experimented with homosexuality to break my pride, to open myself to the story" (61). One reading of this paragraph could be that, for Brodkey, experimenting with homosexuality was a way of understanding and reciprocating his father's desire for him. His pride forced him to deny his father's advances, and by returning the desire of other men, he can rectify what he apparently sees as excessive pride (a pride that needs to be broken). To tell this story more openly would mean conveying the facts, focusing on what can be documented and on those items that best create a narrative. The Brodkey method, in contrast, focuses on experience and feeling, on the peripheral and the invisible. But more importantly, telling the story honestly would mean changing his mind about what is real and what is possible; it would mean providing a definitive story, which he is still unwilling to do. In *This Wild Darkness* Brodkey's style moves toward clear definition, but he continually avoids directness with meta-textual comments and evasions.

We see here that, in Lacanian terminology, Brodkey is caught in the *vel* of alienation. He must choose between the alienated fixity of his public persona and the unity provided by the images of his parents and his fiction. Alienation emerges when he takes his place in the world; separation follows when he attempts to realign his desire with that of the Other. He can only maintain both functions in an imaginary world, and therefore Brodkey's fiction resembles the object *a*; his fictional world provides the *jouissance* of the lost unity. How, then, can a memoir—a representation of what really happened—compare to this? What pleasure does the writing of a memoir provide?

I have suggested that Brodkey's AIDS diagnosis limits his ability to play with these childhood stories. It institutes the "paternal function," disrupting imaginative unity and forcing Brodkey to engage with a world from which he was previously protected. And I believe it does this on several levels. First, the physical discomfort of illness strips him of the protection of his imagination. His body continually reminds him of its presence; he cannot think the pain away. Second, by contracting a terminal disease, and a sexually transmitted disease, Brodkey has, in his mind, literally neutralized the sexual desire of others for himself.[12] Furthermore, he now will join his relatives in death, and therefore he has no need to imagine his identity through them or to keep them alive. Terminal illness has, in fact, enacted the "subjective destitution" that allows Brodkey to acknowledge and traverse the fundamental fantasy of his irresistibility that was maintained by Silenowicz and the Brodkey myth. Although devastating and disruptive, Brodkey illustrates how the AIDS diagnosis frees him from the Other's desire, allowing him to stop the work of protecting himself and to enjoy his immediate present.

The separation from the desire of the Other precipitated by Brodkey's illness helps explain the sense of relief, described earlier, with which the memoir is permeated. Brodkey mentions his exhaustion frequently within the memoir and in the sense that Brodkey felt that he held reality together through his efforts and self-determination, it appears that AIDS has removed the responsibility of keeping danger at bay. Žižek explains that this constant effort is "the typical strategy of the obsessional neurotic, which also involves a 'false activity': he is frantically active in order to prevent the real thing from happening" (1997, 115). For Brodkey, death—the real thing—has now appeared, dwarfing the critics and admirers who have demanded his time and attention in the past. Like Hamlet, Brodkey feels that he has lived according to the time and demands of the Other. And like Hamlet, the death blow allows him to act instead of simply imagining actions.[13] This combination of despondency and freedom is, I suggest, the source of the paradoxical quality of Brodkey's memoir. He begins by stating, "This is how my life ended. And my dying began" (1996, 4). However, it feels at times that in dying Brodkey is actually more alive, or at least alive in a different way: "Attentive to nothing but breath, perhaps in my dying I was alive in a real and complete way, a human way, for the first time after ten or fifteen years of hard work" (1996, 11).

This combination of sadness and relief also appears in Brodkey's public announcement of his diagnosis. Despite the warnings of his doctor and a clear understanding of the stigma of AIDS, he announced his condition in an article entitled "To My Readers," which appeared on June 21, 1993, in *New Yorker*, which begins with the startlingly direct sentence "I have AIDS." The speed, bluntness, and method of direct address all imply an eagerness to share this information. This is particularly interesting because mystification has been a central part of Brodkey's own mythology and an important part of his evasion of the attention of others. Brodkey's eagerness reveals a shift in the way he relates to others and suggests that he is no longer procrastinating. The public statement thus serves as a means of formally separating from the role (and fantasy structure) of irresistible object that he has spent his adult life maintaining.

The End of the Game

What is particularly striking at the beginning of *This Wild Darkness* and in the *New Yorker* articles is the sense of relief with which they are permeated:

> To be honest, the effort of writing, and then my age, and
> the oppressive suffocation of the illness itself, and my sad

conviction of the important validity of my ideas (of what my work represents), and my hapless defense of that work has so tired me that I was relieved by the thought of death. (1994, 71)

Life, particularly Brodkey's writing life, is revealed as a very real battle, despite his claims of detachment from the world's values. His disagreement with those values no doubt intensified his desire to see his own representations praised and accepted. The immediate question the previous quotes raise, however, is why Brodkey felt that the future was his responsibility in the first place, and why he did not simply opt out of the literary games.

To understand Brodkey's previous investment in the world, I will use two texts: Lacan's discussion of Shakespeare's *Hamlet*, and Georg Lukacs's description of the novel of romantic disillusionment in *The Theory of the Novel*. Both texts explore the combination of a righteous idealism with an inability to act—a willful retreat into the self—that permeates Brodkey's pre-AIDS life and art.

In *The Theory of the Novel*, Lukacs (1971) divides the novel into two categories, abstract idealism and romantic disillusionment. Jameson describes the opposition as one between matter and spirit. The hero of the novel of abstract idealism "is characterized by a blind and unshakable conviction in the world's meaning, by an unjustified and obsessive faith in the success of his quest in the here and now, in the very possibility of reconciliation" (1971, 174). In contrast, the novel of romantic disillusionment emphasizes the soul and the subjective consciousness of the hero. "Its hero is passive-receptive, contemplative, and his story is forever on the point of dissolution into the purely lyrical and fragmentary, into a series of subjective moments and moods in which genuine narration is lost" (176). Thus both types present methods of reconciling the discrepancy between the individual's conception of the world and the actual objects the subject encounters. In the extreme of abstract idealism, the hero trudges on enthusiastically, refusing to acknowledge misconceptions and disappointments. The hero of romantic disillusionment, in contrast, sees only disappointment in the world, and therefore he retreats from it into his own consciousness and imagination.

In form and effect, Brodkey's fiction fits amazingly well into Lukacs's category of romantic disillusionment. The events of his stories and novels are structured by the mind of the hero, a mind that follows its own logic in presenting one meaning-filled moment after another. Jameson describes the novel of romantic disillusionment as "menaced by solipsism," and this is a common accusation of Brodkey's critics.[14] We see in *This Wild Darkness* that the fundamental disappointment experienced by his alter ego, Wiley Silenowicz, is also shared by the author, Harold Brodkey. Because he believes the world has been arranged to frustrate his desires, Brodkey uses his will and imagination to subvert that reality through writing fiction. Hence, Brodkey's fictional and actual worlds are set in opposition to each other. The lack experienced in the physical world motivates the fiction, which in turn highlights the world's lack. It is a dialectic without synthesis.

According to Lukacs, when the self becomes the ideal and the world the hurdle to overcome, the result is lyricism:

> The self, cut off from transcendence, recognises itself as the source of the ideal reality, and, as a necessary consequence, as the only material worthy of self-realisation. Life becomes a work of literature; but, as a result, man becomes the author of his own life and at the same time the observer of that life as a created work of art. Such duality can only be given form by lyrical means. As soon as it is fitted into a coherent totality, the certainty of failure becomes manifest; the romanticism becomes sceptical, disappointed and cruel towards itself and the world. (1971, 118)

For Lukacs, the demands of narrative, linear time, and so-called realistic portrayals of objects and behavior frustrate the romantic sensibility. The question of narrative is "What did you do?" or "What did he do next?" The hero of a Brodkey story, in contrast, rarely acts, and therefore such questions are irrelevant; instead, he answers the question "What did you feel or think?" Thus the process of describing those feelings separates Brodkey from the immediate experience of life and what Lukacs would call the "coherent totality" of life.

The duality and its inherent difficulties become evident in a non-fiction essay Brodkey wrote in 1994 entitled "The One Who Writes." Here he describes the pain that his writer-self, who is always turning life into art, causes for his mundane self:

> I can describe him in moonlight, relieved not to have to imagine the moonlight, not to have to phrase it, the silly moonlight, not to have to imagine the city street, the tight row of town houses, the windows, but to have it all be there, solidly there to the senses—he likes to be free of me.

> The unimagined world intoxicates that realer self, and I
> am—it is clear—a twist that his life has taken that he often
> dislikes. (1999, 326)

The split in Brodkey's identity becomes tangible in the pronouns of this passage, as the "I" refers to his writing self and the he or "him" describes the ordinary man walking down the street. The ordinary man is "relieved" not to have the responsibility of creating an aesthetic world. But left alone in the world, the man becomes "intoxicated," which implies stimulation and excitement as well as its Latin root *intoxicare*, to poison. If we take *intoxicated*'s common meaning, perhaps replacing it with the colloquial "drunk," then the word suggests a vulnerability and a lack of control that threaten the writer-self. The drunk man slurs his words, speaks to strangers, and does things he would not normally do, and he often awakens and responds to unwanted desires. All of these behaviors suggest an engagement with the world from which he must be protected. Thus the momentary relief created by the author's absence is threatened by instability, and he must return to the arduous work of creating his life in language.

This paragraph on its own suggests that these two selves, the one who writes and the one who is written, provide a happy, self-sufficient balance of work and play. As several of the previous quotations show, however, the world keeps encroaching on the relationship of "I" and "him." Lukacs sees this intrusion as unavoidable: "An interiority denied the possibility of fulfilling itself in action turns inwards, yet cannot finally renounce what it has lost forever; even if it wanted to do so, life would deny it such a satisfaction; life forces it to continue the struggle and to suffer defeats which the artist anticipates and the hero apprehends" (1971, 118). Here Lukacs implies that a solution to this dilemma would be to renounce what one has lost forever, although he believes that this is impossible. But what is the thing that is lost forever, and what is this "life" that forces it to continue? In Brodkey's case, he believes that he has lost forever a childhood unity by being orphaned at age two, and that loss was reinforced when he was orphaned again as a teenager. Although he accepts the physical reality of the loss of his parents, he keeps them alive in such stories as "Ceil" (his birth mother), "Largely an Oral History of My Mother" (his adoptive mother), and "S. L." (his adoptive father), as well as in *The Runaway Soul*. As romantic author and hero, Brodkey is able to maintain imaginary, fictional relationships, and he is able to create moments of unity that actual circumstances would frustrate.

The struggle to create that unity is centered in language, but the defeats come from the outside world, primarily from literary critics and reviewers, who challenge the validity of his visions and disturb this compensation for his very real and symbolic loss.

Another paradigm that Brodkey's narrative evokes is that of Hamlet, the melancholy orphan whose father is not dead to him and who keeps him alive through his behavior (his excessive mourning) and through art (the staging of a play). Psychoanalytic literature has frequently turned to Shakespeare's play as a classic example of the connection between unfinished mourning and the inability to act.[15] Hamlet could be called, among other things, a disillusioned romantic. In "Desire and the Interpretation of Desire in *Hamlet*," Jacques Lacan describes Hamlet's melancholy in terms of his attachment to the desire of others, and explains that Hamlet cannot act because, "Whatever Hamlet may do, he will do it only at the hour of the Other" (1982, 18). Hamlet, the central character of the play, is constantly caught in other people's stories and must leave his story in the hands of Horatio. He is not able to replace the *Es* with *Ich* until he knows he is about to die and has nothing to lose.

The genre types described by Lukacs and the processes that establish the subject—alienation and separation, proposed by Lacan—blend together at certain points. Lukacs's abstract idealism corresponds to alienation, in that both emphasize the strength of the symbolized world. In both, the subject is dominated by the signifier. Romantic disillusionment resembles separation, in that the power of the signifier is diminished in comparison to that of the subject. Indeed, the signifier gains its significance from the subject, who is able to provide what it lacks. By discussing both Lukacs and Lacan, I hope to establish a connection between genre and psychological process that will help elucidate the difference between the novel and the memoir.

In his book *Jacques Lacan: The Death of an Intellectual Hero* (1983), Stuart Schneiderman develops an idea presented by Robert Jay Lifton, that instead of focusing psychoanalytic symbolization on sex and sexual relations, psychoanalysis might focus on symbols of continuity and discontinuity, or continuity and death (52). In that case, the rivalry between father and son or between brothers would not be for a sexual object but would instead be in terms of the best offering to the dead. Thus Schneiderman replaces the Oedipus myth with the story of Cain and Abel.

Such currency with the dead is present in *Hamlet* and in Brodkey's own mythology. Much of Brodkey's fiction could be described as conversations with the dead; he claims that his dead father instigated his investigations into homosexuality, thereby determining much of his romantic and sexual life; and his status as an orphan dictates his attitude toward all of life's events: "This may be a sense of human style in an orphan, greatly damaged and deadened, a mere sense of style overriding a more normal terror and sense of an injustice of destiny" (1996, 22). The presence of the dead in Brodkey's life story suggests that he has not made peace with them, and that his ongoing relationship with that absence has determined his "style" and distance from the norm. Schneiderman explains how the dead continue to be real to us through the unconscious:

> Unfortunately our passion for science and rationality has prevented us from appreciating the role the dead play for the living. The way we reconcile ourselves with the dead, the way we make peace with them, negotiate with them, determines the quality of our experience insofar as we "ex-sist," insofar as we are situated in another realm from theirs. We usually think of the dead as phantoms and ghosts, to which no mature adult would lend credence. They become relegated to the world of children, infidels, and savages, these ghosts. But as the affair of children, they come to inhabit the unconscious, and Freud identified the unconscious with the infantile. (1983, 76)

For Lacan, the dead, like the gods, inhabit the register of the real. We only encounter them when we diminish our own perceptual consciousness, when we feel disconnected from the physical world. Brodkey requires protection from the world so he can continue his conversations with the dead, both in his fiction and daydreams.

Part of the arrangement Brodkey has negotiated entails keeping the dead alive so he will be invulnerable to so-called normal fears and aspirations, as we see in his fearlessness about death and his invulnerability around people: "Having accepted death long ago in order to be physically and morally free to some extent, I am not crushed by this final sentence of death, at least not yet, and I don't think it is denial" (1996, 19). Brodkey has so little difficulty with death because it is a precondition of life as he knows it. Accepting the physical death of his parents allows him to keep them alive in the space between two deaths, and the imaginary love his parents provide is unending; this frees him from the physical and moral demands of other people.

If, as Freud (1960) suggests in *The Ego and the Id*, the ego is constituted from the traces of objects that have been lost or given up,

then it is possible for the ego to desire itself or to see these incorporated memories/traces as a form of satisfaction. Thus as in the
state of romantic disillusionment described by Lukacs, the subject,
faced with the disappointment of the physical world (the lost object),
recreates an idealized, self-sufficient world through imagination and
consciousness. If time could be made to stand still, then this structure of desire would be less vulnerable; therefore, the subject avoids
action in an attempt to make time stop. Schneiderman explains that
the procrastinator's desire is not of this world; it is of the dead who
are present in the ego:

> The structure of procrastination is that the ego wishes to
> make desire into an ego function, wants to make desire its
> own. Once the lost object is taken into the ego, it becomes
> coextensive with the ego and the ego thinks that what the
> id desires is precisely the ego itself, not the trace of a lost
> object. The ego then thinks that it is loved and that being
> loved is what it desires, as Freud told us, but it goes one
> step further and declares that being loved is all that is
> wanted, that in being loved desire is satisfied, which suc-
> cessfully parries the desire of death. (1983, 149)

The process of turning desire into an ego function sheds light on
Brodkey's proclaimed fearlessness of death, his procrastination and
difficulty publishing, and the structure of his irresistibility, which is
also an aversion to the desire of the Other. From this perspective,
Brodkey's statement that he "never existed except as an Illinois front
yard where these things play themselves out over and over again,"
does not seem quite as hyperbolic.

Part of Brodkey's pride, his "egomania," derives from what he
sees as his past ability to cheat death. Thus his identity is founded
on a recognition that death exists:

> I have had little trouble living with the death-warrant aspect
> of life until now. I never denied, never hysterically denied
> the reality of death, the presence and the idea of it, the
> inevitability of it. I always knew I would die. I never felt
> invulnerable or immortal. I felt the presence and menace of
> death in bright sunlight and in woods and in moments of
> danger in cars and planes. I felt it in others' lives. Fear and
> rage toward death for me is focused on resisting death's

soft jaws at key moments, fighting back the interruption, the separation. In physical moments when I was younger, I had great surges of wild strength when in danger—mountain climbing, for instance—or threatened in a fight or by muggers in the city. In the old days I would put my childish or young strength at the service of people who were ill. I would lend them my willpower, too. Death scared me some, maybe even terrified me in a way, but at the same time I had no great fear of death. (1996, 17–18)

Brodkey's fear of death, unlike the utopia of American advertising he despises, is not rooted in death's denial. Having been so intimate with death as a child, he senses death's constant presence, one that he believes he has avoided through his own power and will. Neither fate, nor luck, nor some transcendent force protected him from life's hazards, but his own strength has kept him alive. Indeed, he believes his strength and willpower kept others alive, including his adoptive parents. Clearly this independence is also a terrifying responsibility, and it reflects Brodkey's need for self-sufficiency and his requirement that, as much as possible, he alone satisfy his needs and desires. Thus although Brodkey does not deny the existence of death, he exalts his ability to fight it, and his relief at giving up this constant fight for himself and his imaginary representations becomes understandable.

A paradox that emerges from both Brodkey's story and *Hamlet* is how the struggle with death becomes an *inactive* struggle. Slowing down time, manipulating time, exactly as Brodkey does in his fiction, emerges as a method of cheating death. Schneiderman describes the rationale behind this strategy: "Thus he procrastinates, and the sense of this procrastination is to slow down the count, to create a duration, a flow of time in which there is no count, in which nothing counts" (1983, 145). Procrastination, like romantic disillusionment, is a denial of the outer, active world in favor of the manipulations of consciousness. To send his stories out into the world would mean submitting them to the reality testing of others, as well as ending the pleasure of inhabiting the imaginative space. This reality testing is clearly difficult for Brodkey, as his hostility toward his critics reveals. But more importantly, writing down his thoughts in finished form demands that he define them and thereby surrender control of this particular dialogue. Completing a written composition, even one of abstract lyricism, is a partial admission of the constraints of time, or, in other words, a submission of the will to the power of death.

Separating from the Ghosts

How does terminal illness enable Brodkey to abandon his need to convince the world of the rightness of his vision and ideas? Why not reassert his will and die in the family tradition of anger and rage? Hamlet acts only when he has been fatally wounded. He knows he has only minutes to live, and therefore his actions do not risk his identity or his connection to his father—they are already gone. As Lacan points out, Hamlet can only act when he has lost his narcissistic attachments, but Hamlet's loss was involuntary and therefore lacking ethically. Using a different metaphor, Schneiderman believes that the ego that idealizes past love attachments can only participate fully in life when the dead have been properly mourned, when they have been symbolically relegated to their proper place. In Brodkey's case, his circumstances are also involuntary. Terminal illness presents him with a consciousness of death and a power greater than his imaginary unity. But this alone might have forced him into a greater despair, a void more terrifying than the previous lack. When Brodkey's initial attack of pneumocystis debilitates him, he is surprised by the willingness of others to come and help. Stripped of will and strength, he is forced to allow the care of others, and, as a consequence, he discovers a new compensation that enables him to finally bury and mourn his past.

I have not found a Brodkey story based on his second wife, Ellen Schwamm, which suggests a difference between Brodkey's use of autobiography in his fiction and in his memoir. In his descriptions of her in *This Wild Darkness*, she appears as his tether to the world, the person who is able to organize people and situations. If Brodkey sees himself as having no coherent self, then Schwamm is the opposite. "She has an identity, of the real, familied sort" (1996, 35) and is his "human credential" (8). "Familied" and "credential" in this context suggest that Schwamm is closer to the symbolic, in contrast to his own life in the imaginary with his fiction and ghosts. Brodkey's descriptions expose an optimism in Schwamm that balances his own pessimism: "I tell her we are cowards and artists and are in flight and are and have to be awful people to get our work done. She ignores me when I talk this way. She does and does not believe what I say or what I believe. "I cannot live like that," is what she says. I mean, I can see, often, the degree of *enlistment* in her being with me" (36 emphasis in original). To what cause is Ellen enlisted? In a general way, it is the cause of meaning in the world, of the world of human action. And the aforementioned discussion indicates a comfortable dialogue based on the acceptance of difference. Schwamm is able to both "believe and not believe" Brodkey's ideas, which perhaps means that she understands how they apply to him but does not believe that they apply to her. Indeed, their different outlooks equip them as a well-suited team. He provides her with a project, reinforcing her connection to the world, while at the same time reminding her of death and sorrow so she is not dominated by the frivolous. She, through her organization and "omnipotence," protects him from the world, but with her hope and faith she also prevents him from falling into complete despair. The drama and power of the first section of *This Wild Darkness* (1996) and of "Dying: An Update" (1994) are determined by Schwamm's role in the narrative. Faced with the final negation of death, the question raised is whether Brodkey will finally join the ghosts of his past or choose to stay with his wife, despite his debilitated state.

The reader gets a sense of this dilemma as Brodkey first reacts to the AIDS diagnosis: "I was ashamed toward her, and angry at her. She does not steadily believe that I love her—it is one of her least endearing traits to expect proof at unreasonable intervals. And what is love? My measure of it is that I should have died to spare her. Her measure is for us to be together longer" (1996, 10–11). I have suggested that what Brodkey calls his "irresistibility" is also an aversion to the demands of the other, demands that intrude on his own internal dialogue. It resembles Hamlet's repudiation of Ophelia, whose earthly desire intrudes on his relationship with his dead father. We see in the previous quote that this dilemma also exists in Brodkey's marriage. Schwamm keeps at him to reciprocate her desire, that is, to show that he loves her, and he does not comprehend her need. His understanding of expressing love would be to leave her alone, as he would want to be left. She, on the other hand, demands action and the love that is physical and perceptible.

Immediately after describing these competing definitions of love, Brodkey conveys a revelatory moment caused by the physical pains of his pneumonia, in which he moves closer to the physical, human space inhabited by Schwamm:

> I thought I could feel myself being suffocated second by second. What was strange was that all sense of presence, all sense of poetry and style, all sense of idea left me. It was gone, with not one trace, one flicker remaining. I had a pale sense of the lost strength it would take to think or feel a metaphor, and of how distant it was from me. (1996, 11)

This description reveals how much Brodkey's daily existence was connected to his writing, his imagination, and his use of language. "Presence" and "idea" are defined as poetry, style, and metaphor. Forced to do nothing but breathe, Brodkey is able to stop thinking in the Brodkey method (a thinking about thinking), and as a result he feels "alive" and "human." It signals a respite from the many dialogues he has maintained in his ego, because he does not have the physical strength to keep them going. The result is that he feels alone, as if inside a large box, yet peaceful.

Within the story the box changes into a hospital room. We see that although Brodkey attempts to keep up an image of strength, he exposes a new vulnerability to Schwamm, in effect, allowing himself to be loved and risking the threat that a human connection poses to his writerly consciousness and his disillusioned perspective:

> She arrived soon after it got light and had a bed for herself moved into my hospital room.
> She said, in an averted way, "I want more time with you."
> And I said, from within my flattened world, "You're nuts. It isn't that much fun to live. Now. And you know it." I sighed. "But if that's what you want . . ."
> "I do," she said. (1996, 12)

Playing his familiar role, Brodkey emphasizes the meaninglessness of existence. Lacking any greater significance, life is judged in terms of "fun," and even then it is found insufficient. But Brodkey is willing to defer to her wishes because at this moment he is lacking in desire, both for his imaginary past and for an immediate present. The self-will and arrogance that had closed the door to so many suitors, editors, and publishers are absent, allowing his wife to inhabit his protected private room.

It is striking, however, that once Schwamm enters the room she becomes a part of Brodkey's imaginary world and, indeed, engages in discourse with his ghosts:

> She was hostess in the narrow hospital room to my mothers, my mothers' ghosts or spirits, and to the line of fathers, the four millennia of unkillable Jewish males in their conceited stiffneckedness, then to all the dead and dying literary figures, then to all the characters who die in the books I most admire. . . . And she made room for the nurses' aides,

for the interns and the residents, for Barry. I have never seen such intent or such subtle seduction: I cannot even begin to describe the silent promises, the hidden blessing she promised them, she promised them all, the ghosts, too. And Death, standing over me and stirring up the muck that refused to be the bottom in the onslaught of the revolting pneumonia. (1996, 32–33)

According to this description, Schwamm in fact lays Brodkey's ghosts to rest. Playing hostess, perhaps a feminine euphemism for "guard" or "protector," she makes the deals and promises that soothe the characters of his imagination and allow them to go away. Schwamm, who represents the practical world of meaning, brings those skills to Brodkey's world of imagination. My understanding of her "promises" is that she provides a guarantee that he will be loved, and because of that knowledge, the ghosts who have protected him for his sixty years are able to leave him in her care. In this way, the promises she makes are in fact a promise of love to Brodkey himself, but made in a form that allows Brodkey to give up the feelings of guilt and responsibility that accompanied his loss. A promise to his ghosts reveals a true understanding of his being and his needs. Schwamm comforts Brodkey in a way he never expected, because no human would know to comfort his ghosts. Although we do not know what she actually did that Brodkey interpreted as these promises, it seems reasonable that the offering of unconditional love, a love that expects no return from Brodkey himself, implies through its excess a love of those unseen elements that also constitute him. It shows a love of him and a love of his "baggage."

The Pass

In his memoir, Brodkey documents the psychological process of dying; he tells the reader, "This is how my life ended. And my dying began" (1996, 4). Separating the two processes with a full stop, he emphasizes that what he does here, both in life and in his writing, differs from what came before. I have tried to emphasize that what occurs in *This Wild Darkness* is a further separation, also referred to by Lacan as "traversing the fantasy," in which Brodkey places himself in the story. The memoir replaces *Es* with *Ich*, and, somewhat paradoxically, Brodkey claims this extra time as his. In my allusions to *Hamlet*, I suggest that one can also view this process through mourning and burial. When we finish burying and mourning our dead, we can get on with our own story. The dead are not forgotten but put in their proper place.

I add one more perspective on this process: Lacan's proposal of the Pass, a process by which analysts in training finish their own analysis and become certified to analyze patients. Elisabeth Roudinesco (1997) describes the Pass in her biography of Lacan: "The candidate for the pass, who was called the *passant*, had to give evidence about his analysis to two other analysts—the *passeurs*—who had to transmit the content of this evidence to a jury" (1997, 338). The jury then had to decide if the *passant* had given up his or her status as "subject supposed to know," which would signal that the transference had been liquidated, and that the *passant* was free of narcissistic attachments. Only by accepting the events of his own story does the analyst avoid entering into imaginary dialogues with the analysand that reenact stories of his own past. As Schneiderman explains, "The candidate for the pass has been called upon to show not that he can speak in his own person, but that he can speak through others, from another place" (1983, 80). Once the story is told, the *passant* cannot rationalize and qualify or retell the story. He or she must accept the judgment of the *passeurs* and the committee and move on. Schneiderman concedes that this lack of explanation is one aspect that made the Pass unpopular: "It is more fun, more secure, to analyze than to be in the position of the dead" (71). I have described Brodkey's fiction as precisely the type of imaginary dialogue that the analyst attempts to avoid. Thus the Pass becomes a ceremony or ritual that the subject can only perform once he is able to stop the interpretive process. It demands an acceptance of one's history, fate, and limited access to power and truth.

To complete this ritual of ego relinquishment, the analysand must establish a new master signifier that accommodates the desire that had been repressed or attributed to the other (in this case, displaced onto Wiley Silenowicz.) Within Brodkey's memoir, the new master signifier emerges in his relationship with Schwamm. Einat Avrahami astutely points out that Brodkey's renewed connection to Schwamm appears as a fallback onto culturally prescribed values: "Ellen represents an assembly of normative, healthy, decent bourgeois practices. Literally and figuratively, she acts as Brodkey's rescuer—first, from his homosexual past, and, second, from the self-hatred and humiliation of dying from AIDS" (2003, 175). Brodkey's description of their relationship is more complicated, however, in that the post-AIDS period of their marriage suggests an intimacy and a connection absent from their prediagnosis marriage, and this earlier period was, presumably, the period of their greatest social acceptability.

Brodkey's development of his marriage to Schwamm as a new master signifier goes through several stages and encompasses a major narrative line within the memoir. His immediate reaction to his diagnosis is that the marriage sacrament has been dissolved; AIDS has made him unlovable. When Schwamm does not leave, Brodkey is forced to reconfigure his image as an object of desire. His subjectivity is no longer connected to his physicality, or we could say that his "agalma," or object *a*, the element that he believed made him desired by others, is now separate from his body. As he recovers, Brodkey begins to explore this new "extimate"[16] self:

> I felt myself to be thoroughly repellent. I had disowned
> my body now and was mostly pain and odors, halting
> speech and a sick man's glances.... Somewhere in this
> phantasmagoria, Ellen decided to wake me.
>
>   A kiss—how strange her lips felt, and the quality of
> life in them. Of course, I thought, of course. The sense I
> had of her, the sensations; the heat of her skin, the heat of
> her eyes so close to me, everything in her was alive still
> and full of the silent speeches that life makes. She was
> warm and full of responsive motion. My lips and feelings
> had the deadness of a sullen child's.
>
>   I accepted her and her affection as truth, as being as
> much truth along those lines as I was likely to want. This
> meant that by the second week I was home we both realized
> that, in this limited world of mutual watchfulness and of
> unselfishness-for-a-while, this period was for us, in awful
> parody, honeymoonlike, and that this was acceptable to both
> of us, grief or death at the end or not. (1996, 97–98)

The passage is striking for several reasons. First, Brodkey's role as sleeping beauty awakened by Schwamm as prince suggests his willingness to accept a feminine position, a position opposed to the masculinity and independence he frequently professed.[17] Then we see that Schwamm's feelings do not reflect Brodkey's attitudes or actions. She is alive and loving, despite his presence as a dead, sullen child. In the final paragraph, Brodkey shows the acceptance of lack necessary to traverse the fantasy; he gives up his vigilant surveillance. Schwamm's affection is good enough. Brodkey accepts that the world is limited, and they are able to exist in a "for-a-while" present tense. The honeymoon that results reflects the paradox of this period of Brodkey's life. What should be a horrible time is, in fact, a honeymoon, because the space between his autonomous self-image and repressed passivity has been removed. AIDS has created a dynamic with Schwamm that allows him to reconfigure himself as someone who gladly accepts love.

What is particularly interesting about this new ability to enjoy the present is how it affects Brodkey's writing. This late shift from fiction to memoir reflects what I have described as Brodkey's separation from the imaginary world of his fiction, a world that hindered what he calls his "outer life."[18] But Brodkey explains that this kind of autobiography is only possible once he has placed himself in the position of the dead:

> For me, now, real faces, real presences, are not decorated by needs or interests of mine. I think it would be an extraordinary intrusion, a trespass, to describe a real face coldly and what I see written there, death or triumph, hatred and disappointment, madness or escape from madness, curiosity, hidden, lonely love, appetite, and ferocity and wit, or blindness. I prefer to be truthful and clear-eyed about imaginary faces. Or ones belonging to the dead. I have always half-known that the narrator of *The Runaway Soul* would have to die in some sense to himself before he could describe himself lucidly, cruelly, simply. (1996, 139)

By moving Brodkey to the position between two deaths, AIDS has paradoxically enabled him to view a more truthful version of his own life. Separated from the finite games of "real" life, Brodkey cannot expect to rewrite the narrative based on new events, insights, or experiences. This forced ending allows him to stop playing and to convey events clearly and directly, hence the relative shortness of his sentences and the immediacy of his prose in the memoir. The healthy, however, still live within the finite games and the possibility of revision. This is why a written description of the living is a trespass; it would push them prematurely toward the experience of subjective destitution, the recognition that their core attributes are elements of fantasy. In *This Wild Darkness*, Brodkey no longer has to protect himself from that same recognition. Silenowicz, the narrator of *The Runaway Soul*, enabled the frenetic activity that kept knowledge of the abyss at bay. Now that the reality of death has appeared, Silenowicz is no longer necessary. Brodkey can slow down, enjoy, and experience the present without fear.

Early interpretations of "traversing the fantasy" suggested that traversing implied a giving up, allowing the analysand to experience a pure desire.[19] Late in his career, particularly in his 1975–1976 seminar on the symptom/*sinthome*, Lacan acknowledged that fantasy cannot be given up, and that a certain amount of fantasy is necessary to avoid madness. Therefore, Lacan proposed that the subject must *identify* with the fantasy—with the symptom that sustains his being—and this identification is the meaning of "traverse" used by commentators such as Žižek, who focus on Lacan's late period. We see this identification with the fundamental fantasy near the end of *This Wild Darkness* in an entry shortly before Brodkey's death:

> I look upon another's insistence on the merits of his or her life—duties, intellect, accomplishments—and see that most of it is nonsense. And me, hell, I am a genius or I am a fraud, or—as I really think—I am possessed by voices and events from the earliest edge of memory and have never existed except as an Illinois front yard where these things play themselves out over and over again until I die. (1996, 173–74).

Here Brodkey claims his ghosts and his existence as a person dominated by memory. It is not Silenowicz who is possessed by ghosts but Brodkey himself. However, Brodkey does not state that his irresistibility was a projection or something that he consciously constructed. He has not given up his imagination in favor of a kind of harsh, empirical reality. Instead he acknowledges that his life has been determined not only by consciously chosen ideals but also by these unconscious fantasies. He recognizes that this element that seemed to be a part of the Other is really a central part of his own subjectivity. Brodkey's narrative suggests, however, that the traversal of fantasy that rearranged this symptom could not have happened prior to his AIDS diagnosis, because without his imaginative world he would have lost his ability to manage his day-to-day existence.[20]

Thus as an ethical guide, the use of Brodkey's memoir is limited. In his essay on *Hamlet*, Lacan explains that Hamlet kills Claudius only when he knows he is mortally wounded. Before that, he cannot give up his "narcissistic attachments." Similarly, Brodkey is only able to give up the ghosts who have impeded his enjoyment once the void of mortality is forced upon him. *This Wild Darkness* does, however, help us understand how fantasy connects to genre, and how different genres facilitate different kinds of knowledge. Brodkey presents his fiction as a reaction to his traumatic childhood, which included both the oppressive closeness of his parents and his painful separation from them. His memoir is a reaction to his AIDS diagnosis and the recognition of the abyss of death (the wild darkness). Both genres attempt to symbolize something that cannot be represented directly. In the fiction, it is the loss of the family; therefore, in his writing, Brodkey recreates those conversations and connections that he missed or whose significance he failed to acknowledge. In the memoir, the loss is Brodkey's own life, which necessarily turns his attention to himself—on that consciousness that will soon be gone and on the new time constraints imposed on that consciousness. Writing fiction allows Brodkey to keep playing with the characters of his past, which is exactly what he needs to maintain desire but keep it at a safe distance. Writing the memoir, like going through the Pass, allows Brodkey to stop playing. Spurred on by the knowledge that his life is ending, he needs a public act that will relieve him of the responsibility of maintaining his mythology. Just as the *passant* hands his legacy over to the *passeurs* to do with as they wish, Brodkey hands the pieces of his mythology over to the reader to interpret as he or she pleases. Both the Pass and the memoir reveal a willingness to finish one's story and move on.

Memoir demands that the writer use his or her memory of events as a curb to the imagination, thereby sacrificing his or her omnipotence. Similarly, that sacrifice implies an acceptance of those past events. In putting what he claims as his truth in print, the memoirist conveys an acceptance of responsibility and the reader's judgment. Of course, the writer can rewrite the memoir, changing facts and characters, but this would then violate the first parameter of autobiography, as described by Elizabeth Bruss (1980), the parameter of truth value, thereby altering the contract with the reader and moving the text into a different genre. Because of these contractual parameters, the memoir acquires a sense of relevance. Connected to time and space, what it loses in universality it gains in communicability.

It should now be clear that Lacan continually revised his theory of the end of analysis. Identifying with the symptom, adopting the discourse of the analyst, performing the Pass, and traversing the fantasy are four overlapping descriptions of a dramatic shift in one's perspective toward desire. All involve a recognition that the big Other, however it was conceived, does not exist, but the process leading to that recognition is different for each subject; therefore, psychoanalysis cannot be rigidly systemized. The reader of these memoirs can observe the change through the effects described, and the terminal illness diagnosis and death function like the darning egg described by Lacan in Seminar XI: "That object whose very reality is purely topological, of that object around which the drive moves, of that object that rises in a bump, like the wooden darning egg in the material which, in analysis, you are darning—the *objet a*" (1978, 257). We can sense the presence and significance of death in each of these texts, but the pattern woven or written around that presence differs in each situation. Thus we can see why Lacan developed multiple ways of describing the end of analysis, prompting his students to look for this change in unexpected places and in innovative ways.

CHAPTER 5

Modern Frame for the Postmodern Image

Reclaiming the Gaze in Derek Jarman's Modern Nature *and* Blue

I. Modernizing Nature, Altering the Imaginary

In a surprising move for a film director, Derek Jarman encourages his readers and viewers to escape from images: "For accustomed to believing in image, an absolute idea of value, his world had forgotten the command of essence: Thou Shall Not Create Unto Thyself Any Graven Image, although you know the task is to fill the empty page. From the bottom of your heart, pray to be released from image" (1994a, 15). In his written texts, Jarman presents the image as intimately linked to the symbolic order: "The image is a prison of the soul, your heredity, your education, your vices and aspirations, your qualities, your psychological world" (15). Jarman does not view the image as a product of artists creatively making metaphors but as the image that captivates and enthralls, creating structures that shape and oppress the unconscious. Thus at the heart of Jarman's work, particularly in texts such as his memoir *Modern Nature* and his last film *Blue*, is an effort to question the way we relate to images, and thereby to reframe the imaginative lens with which we define the real, the authentic, and the good.

One of the projects of art, and particularly modern art and the avant-garde, is to convey a sense of what lies outside of the images and conventions we experience daily. The proliferation of media in the twentieth century has been associated with the increased streamlining of reality. As J.-F. Lyotard has written, "The challenge lay essentially in that photographic and cinematographic processes can accomplish better, faster, and with a circulation a hundred times larger than narrative or pictoral realism, the task which academicism had assigned to realism: to preserve various consciousnesses from doubt" (1984, 74). Although we now have quick access to images from faraway places and different people, most of the images that Westerners see come out of advertising and popular culture with the intention of reinforcing conventional perceptions and identifications. In "Answering the Question: What Is Postmodernism?," Lyotard equates the postmodern with the avant-garde, in that both "continually expose the artifices of presentation that allow thought to be enslaved by the gaze and diverted from the unpresentable" (79). Although both the modern and the postmodern attempt to represent the unpresentable, the postmodern "refuses the consolation of correct forms" and therefore raises the question of whether the created object is indeed art or not. Thus for Lyotard the postmodern precedes the modern because of its disruptive capacity; it may become modern once new forms are established to accommodate the disruption. This placing of the postmodern before the modern is a pattern that continually emerges in Jarman's works, in that the images in his films at first deny categorization. However, Jarman always presents some type of frame that connects the work to "mainstream" culture, whether history, art, or personal narrative, thus tempering the effect of the avant-garde disruption. I believe this technique directly aligns with Jarman's sexual politics, as he continually attempts to show how the "other" is in fact familiar if one adjusts the frame through which it is viewed. By placing the postmodern within the modern frame, he is able to maintain difference while also asserting similarity, and therefore his aesthetics reflect his politics.

Jarman started his career as a painter and set designer and began making feature films in the late 1970s. He remained on the fringe of Anglo-American filmmaking as he consistently challenged conventional ideas of film narrative and cinematography and questioned the goals of modern cinema. To many, Jarman's films were inaccessible and disturbing, and his commercial success was always limited. His position as a public figure altered greatly, however, with the public announcement of his HIV-positive status in early 1987 and his increased participation in the political activism around AIDS. Jarman's artistic perspective was always shaped by his feeling that he was an outsider in British society because of his homosexuality, but his marginalizaiton was reinforced in the 1980s by the conservative government of Margaret Thatcher, the passing of Clause 28, which further stigmatized gays and lesbians, and the rise of antihomosexual sentiment related to AIDS/HIV. Jarman became well known in Britain for combining the aesthetic and political in his work and life, and because of his public availability and prolific autobiographical output, he was a celebrity as much for his approach to life as for any individual work he produced. Although it could be argued that all of Jarman's work is autobiographical, he wrote four expressly autobiographical works between 1984 and his death in 1994: *Dancing Ledge* (1984), *The Last of England* (1987), *Modern Nature* (1991), and *At Your Own Risk: A Saint's Testament* (1992). In many ways the four books form one larger text, as similar events appear in all four volumes but are reshaped to fit the particular ambitions and generic emphases of the individual text.

Much of the originality of Jarman's work derives from his belief in the truth of the individual, momentary experience and his conviction that personal experience can be synthesized into art and society as a whole. The imagery of Jarman's films and the poetry embedded in his prose point toward a world unfettered by the usual contingencies of human perception and social boundaries. At the same time, the material for these images is taken from very real and immediate concerns, and an odd, somewhat perplexing tension is created as the reader's mind moves between these two realms. For example, Jarman's 1990 film *The Garden* juxtaposes images of himself as a child in his father's home movies with sequences of the Virgin Mary (played by Tilda Swinton) running, with the baby Jesus, from paparazzi terrorists. The images rarely have a clear allegorical meaning, but they create a temporary experience for the viewer, an experience that, if effective, alters one's understanding of such concepts as "truth" and "reality" as well as icons such as the home, the Virgin Mary, and the press. Particularly in his films, Jarman creates moments of separation from the dominant symbolic structure as we view elements of his imagination, but that moment's fleetingness emphasizes its frailty and eventual passing.

As I previously suggested, symbolic structures provide a certain amount of meaning to existence, but death challenges the meaning of our worldly accomplishments, and therefore terminal illness often instigates the process of detachment from those structures. Terminal illness forces us to question our significance. As a result, the subject moves back and forth between relatively stable ego certainties (meaning) and desires that transcend the familiar (being). This circular conception of the subject is particularly useful when analyzing Jarman's work, because it reflects his position in between two worlds. In his memoirs, Jarman moves back and forth from concrete descriptions of his daily life to poetic escapes from that life, a movement that also reflects a shift from finite games to infinite games. I would argue that Jarman interested the British public precisely because of his willingness to shuttle between different experiences of being: the old and the new; the pastoral and the urban; the canonical and the avant-garde.

The way in which Jarman emphasizes subjective and momentary experiences brings a heightened political significance to the processes of alienation and separation outlined by Lacan in *Seminar XI*. If we view alienation as a movement toward a symbolic order and fixity of the subject within that order, then it acquires conservative connotations. The lack within that order that the subject attempts to fill in separation counters the rigidity of the law with the variety of desire, revealing separation's subversive element and its dialectical possibilities. Thus it is possible to associate alienation with realism and the status quo. In Jarman's work the status quo is an oppressive force, one that terrorizes gay people, oppresses desire, and separates the powerless from pleasure. In contrast, separation is a positive political move in that it exposes what symbolic structures cannot accommodate and where society does not work—the lack in the Other. The emergence of HIV and AIDS in Jarman's life, and hence in his work, alters and broadens the ways in which he represents the unknown in both his writing and his films. When faced with terminal illness, Jarman moves from words and images that challenge ideas of the ordinary and acceptable in British culture to words and images that challenge our assumptions about death, disease, and existence. And, after disturbing us with unusual images, hidden facts, or culturally repressed desires, he places these items in a personal narrative that humanizes them and makes them accessible.

Modern Nature

> It was very important to find the "I"; *I* feel this, this happened to *me*, *I* did this. I wanted to read that. My obsession with biography is to find these "I"s. The subtext of my films have been the books, putting myself back into the picture. (Jarman 1993a, 30)

Jarman's response to learning his sero-positivity was to buy a small cottage on Britain's south coast at Dungeness. His life after the purchase of Prospect Cottage is documented in his third-volume of autobiography, *Modern Nature*, or, as it was originally published in

Great Britain, *Modern Nature: The Journals of Derek Jarman*. This book chronologically documents Jarman's life from January 1989 to September 1990. The chronology is disrupted, however, by flashbacks to Jarman's past, prompted by associations from his daily life. The image one has of Jarman before the move to Dungeness is of an extremely urban personality. He lived in an apartment on Charing Cross Road in central London. His considerations of the house, garden, and coastline introduce a new solitariness into his life that is reflected in his use of the journal form.

In an insightful essay on Jarman's written work, Matt Cook observes: "There is a sense of literary and physical escape in *Modern Nature* and the garden it depicts. It is not a retreat into the past but into a re-affirming concurrent time where thoughts, associations and life itself are not subsumed by a domineering linear track" (1996, 109–10). What I find of particular interest in Cook's statement is the term "concurrent time" and its suggestion of separate but overlapping experiences of time. If Jarman wants to escape the "domineering linear track," evident in his disdain for narrative throughout his career, then how does a small cottage on a bleak shingle beach with a clear view of a nuclear power plant compensate for the lost security of his urban life?

In trying to formulate an answer, we might begin with Jarman's immediate reaction to learning his HIV-positive status. In an often-repeated anecdote, he writes:

> When the doctor first told me I was HIV positive, I think she was more upset than me. It didn't sink in at first—that took weeks. I thought: this is not true, then I realised the enormity. I had been pushed into yet another corner, this time for keeps. It quickly became a way of life. When the sun shone it became unbearable. I didn't say anything, I had decided to be stoic. This was a chance to be grown-up. Though I thought I ought to be crying. I walked down Charing Cross Road in the sunlight, everyone was so blissfully unaware. The sun is still shining. (1994b, 151)

At first Jarman predictably denies the information given to him as he is still absorbed by the life he constructed around common ideas of mortality. As he adjusts to his diagnosis, however, he places it in the same context as other obstacles he has faced, those things that have kept him from the mainstream, or in the "corners." The sun becomes unbearable because of its indifference to the individual; it has failed to provide the proper lighting and backdrop for the movie that is his life, just as the people on the street remain oblivious to their role in this picture. The key to this entry, however, is the shift in tense of the last sentence. Writing in the immediacy of the present, Jarman transforms the sun from a source of pain to a means of reassurance. It no longer mocks his mortality but emphasizes forms that transcend the individual and that are part of the constancy of nature. Thus in one respect, the alteration in time that Jarman experiences at Dungeness represents an escape from the material time of meetings, lunches, and deadlines but also embraces a concept of time in which loss is part of a natural process that extends beyond his individual experience.

My reading of this last sentence is shaped by the entries following it, just as the collision of the images of a film montage shapes their individual meanings:

> Drako said that as a child he had watched a beautiful blue damselfly emerge from its chrysalis, watched for hours as it unfurled its wings; and then, when it finally took flight, a bird swooped down and scrunched it up. The memory horrified him to this day.
>
> ~
>
> The swallows swoop over the garden catching flies. (1994b, 152)

The displeasure Jarman's friend expresses over the death of the damselfly is a horror over both the fleetingness of beauty and a dismay that the (often miraculous) efforts of life come to such inconsequential endings. That Jarman has placed himself in a position to watch this process daily and expresses no horror at it indicates, if not an acceptance, then at least a desire to experience these life cycles. The bird eats the damselfly despite its beauty, just as the sun shines on Jarman whether he is HIV positive or not. They are images of powerlessness, but the images also evoke greater cycles of development and loss. Thus moving to the coast puts Jarman in greater proximity to death, but also closer to regeneration. Jarman does not turn the damselfly into a direct metaphor for loss but simply presents the image. He does not explain loss, he provides proximity to it.

The primary symbol of this cyclical conception of time and existence in *Modern Nature* is, of course, the garden, which is also the title for the film Jarman makes while keeping these journals. *The Garden* and *Modern Nature* are companion texts: the journal helps explain the images of the film and reinserts Jarman as its primary character. Jarman describes how a personal mythology appears in his writing as well as in his painting and film work; with *Modern Nature*, gardening becomes a central part of his public mythology. Indeed, one could characterize Jarman's *oeuvre* as a process of counter-mythologizing, in an attempt to make himself and his vision *seen* by the world around him:

> A personal mythology recurs in my writing, much the same way poppy wreaths have crept into my films. For me this archeology has become obsessive, for the "experts" my sexuality is a confusion. All received information should make us inverts sad. But before I finish I intend to celebrate our corner of Paradise, the part of the garden the Lord forgot to mention. (1994b, 23)

Here we see how Jarman connects his politics and aesthetics to his sexuality. Creating a personal mythology becomes an obsession for him, because the available mythologies—those endorsed by the experts—do not reflect his experience of himself. Thus he asserts his position in the corner and attempts to turn that corner into Paradise, thereby making visible, and by association real, what was simply his subjective experience. The mythologizing serves a general purpose, but the information he provides about particular objects (such as poppies and the garden) offers insight into the more specific needs that these incorporations satisfy.

The first half of *Modern Nature* stages a detailed exploration of the role gardens played in Jarman's childhood, and the rest of the book documents the transformation of that early cathexis in the events of his later life. Within this context, gardens and flowers represent Jarman's initial contact with the alternative concepts of time and the existence of other worlds:

> Flowers spring up and entwine themselves like bindweed along the footpaths of my childhood. . . . These spring flowers are my first memory, startling discoveries; they shimmered briefly before dying, dividing the enchantment into days and months, like the gong that summoned us to lunch, breaking up my solitude.
>
> The gong brought the pressing necessity of that other world into the garden where I was alone. In that precious time I would stand and watch the garden grow, something imperceptible to my friends. There, in my dreaming, petals

> would open and close, a rose suddenly fall apart scatter-
> ing itself across the path, or a tulip lose a single petal, its
> perfection shattered forever. (1994b, 7)

Through this description of his experience in his grandmother's garden, Jarman establishes a link between his early impressions of nature
and his first consciousness of time. The garden exists as a world set
apart, full of "startling discoveries" of unusual beauty and fragility.
Here time is organized around natural cycles: the opening and closing
of flowers, the losing of petals, the dying of plants, and not the clock
(or gong) of human necessity. Hence, in Jarman's childhood natural
time and human time existed concurrently, but they often conflicted.
The garden is a place where he finds solitude, and the gong cuts into
that solitude, demanding he return to the social, organized world of
the house. Jarman believes that he alone perceives the wonders and
changes of the garden, and they become associated with dreaming and
private consciousness. We see here elements of Jarman's imaginary, as
his experience of the garden stands outside of any socially organized
structure of gardening. He is not learning names or pulling weeds.
Jarman then transforms these memories into the symbolism of his
films. Finally he begins to trace the connections between the memories and mythology in his autobiographical writing, not to impose a
narrative line but to understand the permutations of his own desire
and to make these images his own.

Just as his grandmother's garden provided early experiences of
fantasy and imagination, painting takes on this role during Jarman's
school days in a metonymic shift of desire. Without a garden to tend,
Jarman looks to representations ("Van Gogh for a vase of flowers.
Monet for the garden to grow them in") as the nearest substitute:

> The art school became a fortress against another reality,
> a defence against an everyday existence that was awry.
> I filled the moat with flowers—painted flowers, as I no
> longer had anywhere to grow them. My work set itself
> up against the regime of tight little boys in grey with stiff
> upper lips. (1994b, 61)

In the highly regulated world of the English boys' school, Jarman
seeks out his safe corner. As he presents it, the art school/garden
becomes an escape from the structure of authority as well as a space
for imagination and individual vision. In addition, the identity of the
artist suits Jarman's need for control and his penchant for alternative

myth making: "At the art school I established my own totalitarian state—art was frankly admitted to be incomprehensible, or risible, a thin-air fantasy of mad adventurers who'd sooner cut off an ear or sail for the South Seas than enter useful society, score goals or box their mates into bloody submission" (1994b, 60). Thus the feeling of watching something develop first encountered in the garden transfers to the experience of painting, the pleasure of which reinforces his identification with the outsider and his pleasure in control. As Jarman's environment changes, he shifts his desire to accommodate it, thereby finding the overlap between his desire and the dominant structure of the school.

The move from the isolation of painting to the collaborative effort of filmmaking is not surprising when one considers Jarman's move from the strict Canford School to the Slade School of Art in London. At the Slade, Jarman began designing sets and found a sympathetic group of people with whom to work and play. Thus Jarman's descriptions of the sixties emphasize the sense of newness he and his friends brought to London, and he embraces the spontaneity and creativity of the London art scene. They are still on the outside, but as a group they, like most youth cultures, feel they are at the center of excitement and innovation:

> In the sixties the New was still ours, and the media was only just taking its first faltering steps to exploit it. "Being in the know" meant the thrill of entering a secret world. In the colour supplements and media shows of the eighties everything withers—little survives publicity. (1994b, 176)

The mix of art and gay worlds that Jarman experienced in the sixties was able to convey that same sense of otherworldliness that drew him to the garden, but now it involves a group of like-minded friends, and it is *their* world. What links all of these collaborative projects is the development of something new; it is as if Jarman—the alchemist—chooses to bring together certain elements to see what happens. The final product is not as important as the process of becoming. In working with his friends, Jarman was able to replicate the mood and atmosphere of his father's home movies. He maintains the intimacy and security that the home movie provides while replacing the content with his own adult life and alternative way of seeing. As a result, Jarman's early films, like all of his work, are rooted in a personal tradition yet alter specific representations within that tradition. In addition to allowing Jarman creative flexibility, the super 8 camera offered a new medium for Jarman's vision. In an almost literal exchange, Jarman has taken up the position previously filled by his father and grandfather but has altered that position to suit his own conception of reality. Thus through film Jarman finds a means of representing his own vision, filling the lack he feels in tradition and the dominant order. By reshooting the home movie, Jarman has, in a sense, "traversed the phantasy," a process evident in much of Jarman's work.

Rejecting the images of comfortable suburban life in which he was inscribed as a child, Jarman rewrites his story, moving his position from the filmed to the filmer. Whether the shift in content is subtle, as in *Ula's Fete*, which shows a group of friends having lunch, or dramatic, as in the surreal images of *In the Shadow of the Sun*, the scene of becoming is (ostensibly) controlled by Jarman. The super 8 camera keeps him in his corner, a place in which Jarman's identity is now heavily invested, but enables him to define that space in his own terms. Film is the culmination of a chain of alternative visions that began with his childhood wonder in the garden and increased to the public distribution of his vision, alone and in collaboration with his colleagues.

The Movement toward Montage

> This same principle—giving birth to concepts, to emotions, by juxtaposing two disparate elements—led to: *Liberation of the whole action from the definition of time and space.* (Eisenstein 1949, 58, emphasis in original)

Modern Nature shows how Jarman moves back to previous scenes of desire when he discovers his HIV status—not just in memory—but by reenacting former creative actions such as gardening and painting, and in transcribing those actions in the present. Faced with trauma, Jarman retreats even farther from the city and linear time, replacing more ordinary interests with an environment and activities that are able to evoke previous feelings of wholeness or wonder. Terminal illness does not separate Jarman from life but instead propels him toward the origins of his own personal mythology.

The journal format of *Modern Nature* is ideally suited to translate these new experiences of being into a communicable format. The autobiography is retrospective and looks for closure—for an explanation of what happened that implies cause-and effect relationships. In contrast, Jarman's journals document him in the process of living. *Modern Nature* emphasizes individual moments over a coherent narrative structure, thereby delineating the fundamental difference in representations of time in the two formats. Jarman attempts to render the elusive quality of "existence" that the dull repetition of images has deadened. Therefore, in *Modern Nature*, Jarman often does not directly present causal relationships between events in order to solve the mystery of his life. Instead, he brings together those moments when existence is palpable, and he integrates them into the mundane experiences of living in order to elevate life as a whole. Although Jarman follows chronological headings within the journals, each entry splices together disparate subjects and periods. The structure emulates the cinematic technique of montage, forcing the reader to draw the spiritual and thematic connections.

As a consequence, Jarman's style and ideas on art resemble Eisenstein's,[1] as well as many modernist artist and thinkers. His belief that nonrepresentationalism penetrates deeper into existence, his emphasis on the intuitive and the poetic, his distrust of communal notions of reality and causality, his belief in the subjective and the emotional, and his faith in art's ability to shape experience into something new and complete place him squarely in the modernist tradition. Indeed, his attraction to both apocalypse and an idyllic past reflects his connection to the modernist imagination. Jarman's term *"modern* nature" synthesizes his own perspective into the greater, traditional concept of the English pastoral, just as many of his films (*The Tempest, Edward II, The Last of England*) add his perspective to canonical elements of British culture. As leading modernist D. H. Lawrence pointed out, visualizing the unknown entails a distancing from civilization:

> To appreciate the pagan manner of thought we have to drop our own manner of on-and-on-and-on, from start to finish, and allow the mind to move in cycles, or to flit here and there over a cluster of images. Our idea of time as a continuity in an eternal, straight line has crippled our consciousness cruelly. (Bradbury and McFarlane 1976, 52)

Jarman developed the technique of allowing the mind to float over a cluster of images in his super 8 films, and he brings this approach to the prose of *Modern Nature*. As Lawrence implies, this expansion of consciousness entails a *redefinition* of nature (through the pagan), summarizing Jarman's project. He brings together elements in new configurations to both see what happens and to gain control of the scene. Organized by the individual consciousness, the journal synthesizes into Jarman's daily life sexuality, art, and HIV. The annihilating effect of a symbol such as HIV is lessened when placed in discourse with these other elements.

In Jarman's February 24, 1988, entry he presents three sections that represent different aspects of life but are linked in his thoughts to the winter wind. He begins with a realistic description of the weather and his daily activities:

> A grey windy day, cold too. . . . Yesterday I made a rather optimistic expedition to our local nurseries at Greatstone, where plants can be obtained at a fraction of the regular cost, and came away with lavender and rosemary, saxifrage, montbretia, iris, and an ostentatious yucca to crown the lot. (1994b, 18)

The next two sections, however, move to the memory of the Great Storm of the previous year and are spurred by a childhood memory of *The Wizard of Oz*. Jarman transforms Prospect Cottage into Dorothy's house blown by the tornado to the land of Oz. In this section, the wind takes on metaphoric significance as the threatening power of fate and nature, and the cottage becomes the flimsy human constructions that protect us. The house remains intact after the storm, but the original feelings of danger and escape are introduced through the childhood experience of the movie and its effect on Jarman's interpretation of experience.

Jarman speculates that the childhood experience of the film may have initiated a desire that he has now fulfilled: "Without light or heat for the next week, I stared at the glittering power plant on the horizon and wondered if, like the Emerald City and the great Oz himself, my life and this cottage had been dreamt all those years ago in Rome" (1994b, 19). Thus Jarman suggests the great extent to which conscious adult choices are shaped by apparently insignificant childhood experiences. The storm allows him to see the resemblances between the power plant and the Emerald City, his cottage and the Kansas farm, and Dorothy and himself.

Once the memory of the storm has suggested the limits of his own conscious will, Jarman's contemplation of his surroundings carries his thoughts to the metaphysical:

> I live in borrowed time, therefore I see no reason in the world why my heart grows not dark.
> A cold wind blows tonight over this desolate island.

Over the hills and dales, over mountain and marsh, down the great roads and little lanes, through the villages and small towns, through the great towns in cities.

Everywhere it blows through empty streets and desolate houses, rattling the hedgerows and broken windows, drumming on locked doors.

The wind is blowing high in the tower blocks and steeples, down along the river, invading houses and mansions, through the corridors and up the staircases, rustling the faded curtains in bedrooms, over the carpets, up the aisles and down in the crypts, in public places and private, among forgotten secrets, round the armchair, the easy chair, across the kitchen table.

So icy is this wind that it rattles the bones in the graves and sends rats shivering down the sewers.

Fragments of memory eddy past and are lost in the dark. In the gusts yellowing half-forgotten papers whirl old headlines up and over dingy suburban houses, past leaders and obituaries, the debris of inaction, into the void. Thought illuminated briefly by lightning. The rainbows are put out, the crocks of gold lie rusting—forgotten as the fallen trees which strew the fields and dead meadows.

I consider the lives of warriors, how they suddenly left their falls.

Bold and noble leaders,
I shiver and regret my time. (1994b, 19–20)

I quote this passage at length because the repetition and pattern are crucial to its meaning. (In fact, Jarman will continue this section for another page.) The colloquial prose that Jarman used to describe his daily activities has been transformed into a rhythmic, poetic incantation of his psychic state. In the same way that James Joyce uses snow at the end of "The Dead," Jarman uses the wind to bring together parts of Britain separated by landscape, class, and time. The wind as an element of nature stands in contrast to the insignificance and transitory nature of human constructions. A consciousness of mortality has diminished the significance of individual action, and the lengthy list of humanity's detritus only emphasizes our redundancy. In the tradition of modernist symbolism, Jarman uses the wind to suggest what cannot be represented. Like Joyce's snow or Forster's Marabar Caves, the wind suggests a unity of being, but that unity reinscribes its distance from the human and therefore implies death. It transcends subjectivity and what we understand as meaning through discourse. This is reiterated by the style of the prose, whose gaps and indeterminacies draw attention to its incompleteness. In the end, however, the human struggle for good takes on a particular poignancy when considered against these limitations. More idealist than nihilist, Jarman regrets that more cannot be accomplished during his short time on earth.

Thus within the space of one day's entry, Jarman brings together three different ways of experiencing the world—ways that loosely correspond to Lacan's symbolic, imaginary, and real. The first section contains familiar forms of signification. It gives names to objects and places them in a common structure of exchange ("a fraction of the regular cost"). The second section revolves around images, specifically film images, and how early representations shape desire and understanding of truth and reality. Thus Jarman organizes the world first by words, then by images; in the final section, however, the wind emerges as that which is beyond organization. Because of HIV, Jarman lives "in borrowed time," and as he attempts to convey that liminal experience, he resorts to an image that is felt but not seen, and to language that seems to wander without purpose. The undifferentiated plenitude of the wind provides an image of the real, but it evokes the transcendent precisely because of its failure to encompass wholeness. The list of places the wind visits can never be complete, but the *idea* of completion is suggested by that absence. That is the paradox of the real as generated by the symbolic. Just as absence is central to establishing the uniqueness of the garden, absence creates the atmosphere of this passage. It suggests a unifying otherness with its imagery and language and demands that the reader provide the connections between the elements of the montage.

This passage is one of the entries in *Modern Nature* in which the division between Jarman's books and films begins to break down. Whereas previously abstraction was found in Jarman's films and the books retained a fairly conventional approach to explaining his films and activities, here the numinous experience and the individual identity are brought together. Thus in allowing his entries to follow his desire instead of an explanatory narrative, Jarman adds a greater sense of being to the text.[2] When the efficacy of the symbolic order is called into question by terminal illness, the subject will cling even tighter to the permutations that lie beyond it. Jarman uses the journal format to document not only his public self but also the imaginary roots of that self and the influence of the real. The differences in tone and style between these passages evoke the different ways in which humans access knowledge, represented in Lacanian theory by the three registers. Thus the combining of the three registers is similar to the combination of the modern and postmodern in Lyotard's vocabulary, and the diary therefore functions as the *sinthome* as presented in Lacan's 1975–1976 Seminar; it is the fourth ring that connects experiences from the three registers and allows the subject to function.

Projecting and Viewing

Shortly after Jarman's death, I attended a conference at the Institute of Contemporary Arts (ICA) in London, which featured a discussion of Jarman's work and his role in British cinema. One of the participants, John Mayberry (a young filmmaker who worked with Jarman on many small projects), described how Jarman was just as entertained by his diary entries as were his friends who were hearing them for the first time. Mayberry suggested that by writing down his experiences and reading them aloud to an audience, Jarman made the experiences real to himself. Jarman's prolific autobiographical writing, his insistence on the presence of the author in art, and his repetition of specific anecdotes all reinforce the importance that he places on representing himself. His discontent with his preassigned position in this larger symbolic order encourages him to reconstruct himself, a process evident in his many forms of counter-mythologizing already mentioned. Thus I would argue that all of Jarman's work participates in this reclaiming of the symbolic by connecting it to his own imaginary in a public way.

Jarman makes being seen an explicit issue in most of his political writing, and it dominates his later book, *At Your Own Risk*, which mixes documentation of twentieth-century gay culture with Jarman's personal experiences and observations. Representing gay desire also drives Jarman's more narrative-based films such as *Caravaggio* and *Edward II*. Thus two parallel yet related strategies emerge in Jarman's work: positing new ways of presenting images ("the reinvention of my cinema") and establishing a reinterpreted gay history ("the reclaiming of the Queer Past" (1993b, 7). Jarman believes that "heterosoc" continues to demonize gay culture because it refuses to see it: "We are the 11,000 angels dancing on the head of a pin" (1993a, 4). One important part of his project is to bring individuality back to the discussion of AIDS and gay issues, a strategy he believes will humanize the discussion:

The problem of so much of the writing about this epidemic is the absence of the author. How would the much criticised article "Gay Abandon" in the Guardian have read if it were in the first person?

"I am maladjusted," "I am the end of the line." (1993a, 5)

Thus Jarman makes explicit his goal of personalizing what appears in the mainstream as transgressive, particularly in the Thatcher years. If his films expose the artifice of reality as presented through mainstream cinema, then his autobiographies show that his point of view (and therefore his films) is quite ordinary.

In *Modern Nature*, Jarman challenges social propriety with his descriptions of Hampstead Heath and the sexual activity that goes on there. In these passages, which his editor recommended he leave out, he confronts this particular demonization of homosexuality, challenging the assumptions behind those fears and taming the frightening images by personalizing and humanizing them:

Location is the key to respectability, it's like cocaine in the boardroom and the needle of the streets. But for those who know, the alfresco fuck is the original fuck. Didn't the Garden of Eden come before the house which hid our nakedness? Sex on the Heath is an idyll pre-fall. Did Adam masturbate until God hacked out his rib to create Eve?

All the Cains and Abels you could wish for are out on a hot night, the May blossom scents the air and the bushes glimmer like a phosphorescent counterpane in the indigo sky. Under the great beeches some boys with gypsy faces have lit a fire, which they stoke sending sparks flying, smiling faces flushed with the heat. In the dark for a brief moment age, class, wealth, all the barriers are down. An illusion you say, I know but what a sweet one.

... Conversations are brief, though I have talked the night away, here it's quiet, none of the decibels that have invaded every other public space to drown out a conversation.

... Sex these days is as safe as you'll find it, few risk penetration, it's mostly confined to what my mum would call "horseplay." No-one who comes here need leave without an orgasm, though many come to walk and forget the frustrations of the day.

... After a week's absence I have visited the Heath several times recently, it is always exciting and joyous. The deep silence, the cool night air, the pools of moonlight and stars, the great oaks and beeches—all old friends. The saplings I've watched grow to trees forty foot high in the years since I first came in the sixties.

The place has changed, there was a time when any number of friends were out on a warm weekend. Sometimes it almost resembled a garden party, joints were rolled, hip flasks produced. People laughing and shouting, like a midnight swim. In the seventies it became even less inhibited, but, as always, once you are over the invisible border your heart beats faster and the world seems a better place. (1994b, 83–84)

In this passage Jarman draws on a series of images not typically associated with gay culture and uses them to present the Heath in a new way. Primarily, he highlights the wonders of nature in this environment, questioning the "naturalness" of our confinement of sex to the bedroom. In Jarman's description the Heath offers pleasure for all of the senses, thereby constructing an ideal space for the exploration of bodily pleasure. Indeed, the Heath is even seen as superior to the bedroom in its resemblance to an idyllic pre-fall world. As is typical in *Modern Nature*, social constructs separate people from meaningful experience. Jarman redefines gay sex as natural by linking it to the bucolic and images of a precultural Eden.

In addition, Jarman reframes the image of the libidinous homosexual driven solely by the desire for sex. The common tending of a fire, the suggestion of simple conversations, the utter ordinariness of the sex, and the overall tone of friendliness all suggest that instead of being dangerous to the individual and society, the Heath is actually a positive social environment where individuals are respected. The comparison of sex on the Heath to a garden party links it to yet another dominant British cultural image but omits formalities and class restrictions. Hampstead Heath becomes the respectable garden of a communal country house.

Thus by drawing on the familiar cultural references of the pastoral, the Bible, and middle-class social life, Jarman is able to present an image of the Heath that is familiar and unthreatening without replicating the elements of a repressive social order. Presenting the sexuality on the Heath in these terms, Jarman alters the imaginary patterns associated with homosexuals, thus creating the potential for a change in judgment of the group as a whole. According to Lacan, designations of good and bad are determined by an imaginary association of inside or outside. Jarman still crosses the "invisible border," placing himself in his corner, but he presents that corner to those who do not know it as something as familiar as Eden or a country house. It maintains a symbolic distance from the everyday world but gains an ethical approval through its attachment to positive, familiar feeling (the inside).

In other words, Jarman has altered the image/screen through which the reader views sex on the Heath—presenting the unpresentable—while also inscribing himself as the source and perspective of that picture. In 1991, Jarman's visits to and descriptions of the Heath were seen by many as reckless and irresponsible and by others as courageous and honest. Jarman explained his open writing about sex with references to people's unwillingness to discuss the topic, his inability to keep a secret, and his insistence on honesty. But it also exemplifies Jarman's faith and optimism that his personal experience carries a resonance that is communicable to others. Once others view the world through his image screen, they will accept and, ideally, appreciate it.

An interesting congruence appears between Jarman's trips to the Heath and his publication of personal details about his life. One can reasonably posit that one reason for the taboo on public sex developed from the vulnerability to approach and possibility of observation by an unwelcome eye. With the loss of privacy, the absorption or loss of self that comes through sex is destroyed. Like Sartre's person looking through the keyhole, it is commonly assumed that the person having sex feels self-conscious and embarrassed when viewed by the Other. In Lacan's discussion of the gaze in *Seminar XI*, however, he rightly points out that this oppressive gaze is not necessarily a "seen gaze, but [can be] a gaze imagined by me in the field of the Other" (1978, 84). Thus we see in Jarman's memoirs not only a redefinition of himself but a taming of the internalized gaze of the disapproving Other that he links to heterosexual society. This functions in two related ways. First, by providing a perspective for the reader, Jarman guides the reader's gaze in a particular direction. Lacan describes this process through painting, but I believe it is equally applicable to film and literature:

> The painter gives something to the person who must stand
> in front of his painting which, in part, at least, of the paint-
> ing, might be summed up thus—*You want to see? Well, take
> a look at this!* He gives something for the eye to feed on, but
> he invites the person to whom this picture is presented to

lay down his gaze there as one lays down one's weapons.
(Lacan 1978, 101, emphases in original)

To an extent, Jarman is saying to the public: "If you are so fascinated
by gay sexuality (as evidenced by the tabloid press), then look at gay
sexuality from my perspective." Presenting his own experience, Jarman can at least "invite" readers to look at things in the same way he
does. His hope is that the reader will, at least temporarily, lay down
his or her arms and experience a temporary empathy or identification
with him. The momentary identification exposes the variety of ways
in which images can be interpreted and, ideally, weakens the position
of the disapproving gaze.

Second, Jarman tames the gaze by avoiding the Other completely,
or, in other words, by emphasizing the separation between himself as
character, author, and reader so he becomes Other to himself. Lacan
explains that one way of eliding the gaze is in the process of "*seeing
oneself see oneself*" (1978, 74, emphasis in original). It is a momentary
experience in which, paradoxically, the splitting of oneself enables the
desire of the Other to be replaced with one's own desire. The subject
is precipitated in the dialectic of desire created by the two parts, the
subject aspiring to the wholeness present in the main character of the
memoir. Although this is similar to the child viewing his/her own
image in Lacan's description of the mirror stage, it differs in that its
strength derives from the subject's perception of his *active* creation of
himself. The character is shaped by the author, and the person looking down is not the inapprehensible Other of the gaze but the author
as *viewer*. The adult sees himself, dressed in the elaborate costume
he has chosen, in the mirror. In reentering the text as reader, Jarman
replaces the intruding eye not only with his own perspective but with
his own eye.[3] The idealistic hope of convincing an unknown reader
with one's descriptions provides one form of pleasure, but in seeing
oneself see oneself, Jarman has created a self-enclosed system in which
he determines his own image—he is both the looker and the looked
at—providing a much stronger *jouissance*. I suspect that Jarman read
his diaries aloud not only to please his audience but to give pleasure
to himself, to reaffirm his existence.

Transcendent Desire

Writing, filmmaking, and gardening all provide Jarman with opportu-
nities to engage in life and therefore to combat the annihilating effects

of HIV and the public label "AIDS victim." However, *Modern Nature* reflects a subtle shift in his autobiographical work in that it adds a more metaphysical aspect to his observations and commentaries. Although the image of the garden dominates the journals, Jarman's move to Dungeness is also significant because of the presence of sea, sky, and light that he attentively describes. These images function differently from the garden in that instead of bringing Jarman back to an active participation in life, they instigate reflection on what lies beyond the limits of knowledge and experience, often functioning as metaphors for death. As Jonathan Dollimore explains in his essay "Sex and Death," the two types of images express different forms of yearning that are interrelated and possibly cyclical in nature, like alienation and separation:

> *Now* an attempt to flee that sense of separation and incompleteness, a wish for difference without pain, for unity, identity, and selfhood, through union with the other; *now* a desired, even willed loss of identity in which death is metaphor for, or fantasized or the literal event guaranteeing, the transcendence of desire. (1995, 48, emphases in original)

Thus while Jarman describes many experiences that consolidate identity, his descriptions of the landscape also suggest a desire to get beyond that identity and to transcend desire.

Dungeness provides Jarman with many images with which he can explore the idea of physical limits and limit experiences. On the first page of *Modern Nature*, we see that he has chosen this location precisely because of its lack of boundaries and divisions: "There are no walls or fences. My garden's boundaries are the horizon. In this desolate landscape the silence is broken only by the wind, and the gulls squabbling round the fishermen bringing in the afternoon catch" (1994b, 3). By seeking a space without boundaries, Jarman flees meaning that is dominated by the symbolic and the binary signifier. But, more importantly, making the horizon the border of his own garden shows a pleasure in proximity to that limitlessness, or a desire for an image of the real. Lacan suggests that "image is functionally essential for man, in that it provides him with the orthopedic complement of that native insufficiency, constitutive confusion or disharmony, that is linked to his prematurity at birth" (1993, 95). For the ailing Jarman, the ocean's orthopedic function is to enable him to conceive the limitless, which brings him one step closer to imagining death.

Images of limitlessness and transcendence appear frequently but in short passages, usually as introductions to his descriptions of the day in Dungeness. Jarman often begins an entry with a quick sketch of the position of the sun or moon, the quality of the light, and the effect of these conditions on the appearance of the shingle beach and sea. These passages reframe the narrative through this greater perspective. Instead of focusing on the look generated by Jarman's eye, the omnipotent power of the gaze is suggested through the celestial sources of light. These moments contrast with the descriptions in which Jarman tames the gaze through the conventions of social interaction (the literary equivalent of the shot/reverse shot), or through seeing himself see himself. Instead, he is being watched, as if by a benevolent deity:

> From my home I can see the sun clamber out of a misty sea. It wakes me through the bedroom window and then stays with me all day. There are no trees or hills to hide it. When it sets over the flatlands in the west I sit and watch it on a throne-like chair that I rescued from a rubbish dump. I never miss the setting sun, however cold the weather.
>
> Tonight it hangs huge and scarlet after a day of dark clouds. It appears for a few brief minutes, a perfect circle before disappearing—then the darkness comes rushing across the sky to embrace the inky timbers of Prospect Cottage; but before the light is extinguished the house reflects gold, or, as this evening, blazes ruby, its panes of glass a dazzling scarlet. (1994b, 31)

In this scene the set and lighting are not controlled by Jarman but by a supreme force that we could refer to as "nature." Interestingly, however, the language Jarman uses lends to nature the connotation of nurturer, as the sun obligingly awakens him and stays with him, as if in a protective capacity. Moreover, in its perfection, it "embraces" Jarman's house, Prospect Cottage, making it beautiful and, by association, loved. Thus Jarman's move to Dungeness brings a shift in the gaze through which he constitutes himself. The culturally specific activities that defined him in London—film director, artist, activist—are temporarily replaced by the transcendent and beneficent sun.

In the two forms of yearning described by Dollimore in "Sex and Death," we see that the conceptualizing of death entails the search for wholeness not as we experience it through interaction with the Other but in an escape from subjectivity as we know it through that

Other. It is in this guise that death becomes freeing: as a release from the frailties of the ego. If, as Lacan suggests, the ego is rooted in the imago established during the mirror stage, then freedom from the ego also would entail freedom from traditional images, from the imaginary that distinguishes between the inside and the outside. The separation between Jarman as an inhabiter of the earth and the universe beyond breaks down in his descriptions of the night sky from his cottage. Here human and infinite interact, defying classification:

> The night sky here is a riot that outshines the brightest lights of Piccadilly; the stars have the intensity of jewels. So flat is the Ness that those stars that lie at the horizon touch your very feet and the moon tips the waves with silver.
>
> Never in my many sleepless nights have I witnessed a spectacle like this. Not the antique bells of the flocks moving up a Sardinian hillside, the barking of dogs and the sharp cries of the shepherd boys, nor moonlit nights sailing the Aegean, nor the scented nights and fireflies of Fire Island, smashed glass star-strewn through the piers along the Hudson—nothing can quite equal this.
>
> The orchestra has struck up the music of the spheres, the spectral dancers on the fated liner whirl you off your feet till you feel the great globe move. Light-hearted laughter. Here man has invaded the heavens; but the moon, not to be usurped, shines sickle bright, gathering in our souls. (1994b, 52–53)

In this passage Jarman describes a mystical union and takes a risk in using this language. Phrases such as "music of the spheres," "invading the heavens," and "gathering in our souls" are highly ambiguous and will be interpreted differently by many readers. That obscurity, however, suggests that he is at the point where language breaks down—where being cannot be contained by words. And it is precisely because this experience is not culturally reified that it has such a powerful effect on Jarman. Death does not enter the passage directly, but it is suggested precisely through this absence of narrative and boundary. The one consolation of death may be a release from the images and stories that confine us, and the broader scope of vision Jarman experiences on his beach prefigures the possibility of an even broader vision after death—after the doors of perception have been cleansed and the threshold of the visible world is expanded. Jarman's attempt to convey death, inaccessible to our limited imagination and vision, through a new juxtaposition of images follows a pattern that he began when he first picked up the super 8 camera and tried to present his immediate world in a new way. Using his unique vision, he places death, both present and absent, in the story of his life. The postmodern is framed by the modern. The symptom becomes the *sinthome*.

II. The Blind Man's Gaze:
Derek Jarman's *Blue* and the Cinema of Desire

In his landmark essay, "Freud's Masterplot,"[4] Peter Brooks (1984) examines how the plots of novels often follow a Freudian model of the life span, in which one drive moves relentlessly toward the end, while a competing drive creates detours so that the organism does not die prematurely, before its "proper" end. The Freudian masterplot creates problems, however, for many who are sick or dying from diseases such as HIV and cancer, because it seems to suggest that the ill person has failed in his or her duty to avoid the "short-circuits" that life presents. Moreover, Brooks's analysis of the Freudian plot ignores the ways in which culture determines what is a proper end and what is a short-circuit. In response to the dominance of the Freudian plot, Arthur Frank, a scholar of illness and disability, has argued that "Telling an interrupted life requires a new kind of narrative" (58), and in the last twenty years, writers and artists from a variety of backgrounds have answered this call with dramatic innovations in the genre of memoir.

One of the most challenging and inspiring examples of a new kind of memoir is Jarman's final film *Blue*. Released in 1993, shortly before Jarman's death in February 1994, *Blue* presents the viewer with seventy-six minutes of uninterrupted blue screen, accompanied by music composed by Simon Fisher-Turner and lyrical and autobiographical text read by John Quentin, Nigel Terry, Tilda Swinton, and Jarman himself. The film was first conceived in the 1980s as an homage to Yves Klein,[5] but Jarman was inspired to complete the project after losing most of his sight to cytomegalovirus (CMV) retinitis in 1993. Thus the blue screen is meant to convey the experience of blindness, but it also evokes those particular blind spots over which the cultural apparatus cannot gain mastery, such as disease, disability, and mortality. By forcing the viewer to experience the solid-blue screen, Jarman creates for the viewer a momentary displacement that suggests the experience of being blind, disabled, and marginalized. The static screen distances the audience from familiar cultural narratives that dictate how to see and what to think. Looking at the screen, the viewer tries to use the sound track cues to establish fantasy scenarios that will "heal" this disorientation. The attempts provide momentary pleasures, but they are limited by a necessary shifting between the finite world of home and hospital, suggested by the prose passages on the sound track, and the infinite concepts of death and time, evoked by the poetry and the luminous blue screen. This circular movement from one perspective to another emerges as an alternative to the linear plot described by Brooks, and Jarman shows how this constant shifting of frames creates frustrations but also allows access to new forms of enjoyment, such as the film itself.

The powerful effect of *Blue* comes, of course, from the static blue screen. For me, and for many other viewers, the blue screen has a surprisingly disorienting effect, in that although it remains basically the same, images come and go on the screen that make one doubt one's vision.[6] Peter Schwenger describes this disorientation as the "Ganzfeld Effect," a phenomenon first experienced by Arctic explorers confronted with a completely white visual field. Unable to tolerate the undifferentiated field, the mind projects images from memory, confusing inner and outer vision (Schwenger 1996, 420). Through the blue screen, the viewer gets a rare insight into a particular kind of blindness, and the images reveal the active role we play in determining the visual field. In turn, the experience makes one question how much of ordinary reality is simply a construction of the mind, determined by what we need to see.

The self-consciousness that Jarman's film forces on the viewer is addressed by Lacan (1978) in his discussion of the gaze in Seminar XI. For Lacan, the gaze is not a camera eye recording information but a spot or stain that disturbs our safe distance from objects, creating an awareness of our position relative to the outside world. The blue screen functions as the gaze (Lacan even refers to the gaze as a screen), in that we enter the theatre expecting to be passive receivers, experiencing the power of narrative and the cinematic apparatus but, in fact, the static screen does not explicitly tell us what to see or how to look. The blue screen evokes anxiety that leads the viewer to repeatedly wonder what Jarman wants of us and what he is trying to show with this blinding image.

The question "What does he want?" is, according to Lacan, the key to understanding the fantasies we construct to tame the disturbing power of the gaze. The individual wants to understand the desire of the Other (both the big Other of culture and the small other of those around him or her) in order to properly respond to that desire. Not knowing the Other's desire creates anxiety, and fantasy calms that anxiety by providing an answer to the question. One of the pleasures provided by the typical Hollywood movie is unprecedented access to the motivations of others. The seemingly omnipresent camera reveals secrets that we could never discover in real life and, as a result, our fantasies are confirmed and, often, our cultural values are reinforced. Although Jarman's sound track is at times extremely personal and revealing, the blue screen and his use of figurative language and abstraction severely limit our access to him. As a result, viewers want to know more; they desire the "truth" behind the image, but that truth is primarily, as Jarman shows, a projection of the imagination.

Slavoj Žižek's writing on the gaze focuses on this question of what the Other wants from us, which he names with the Italian expression *Che vuoi?*[7] Žižek uses the gaze and *Che vuoi?* to elucidate examples of racist thinking in which one imagines that the Other wants such things as one's money, women, children, and so on. The Lacanian/ Žižekian understanding of the gaze is therefore particularly useful in explaining why Jarman uses the blue screen to block simplistic fantasies about his desire. At this juncture Jarman finds himself different from the mythical norm in (at least) three ways: his homosexuality, his HIV status, and his blindness. These qualities problematize culturally dominant fantasies of sex, romance, and agency, and the viewer is initially engaged by a curiosity to know how Jarman responds to these challenges. The brilliance of Jarman's film lies in his unwillingness to *tell* us exactly what he wants. Instead, he *shows* us how he uses language, sound, image, wit, and the blurring of boundaries between discourses to enjoy living in the here and now.

The opening of *Blue* introduces the viewer to a language that draws on traditional discourses but reframes them in order to create new meanings:

> You say to the boy open your eyes
> When he opens his eyes and sees the light
> You make him cry out. Saying
> O Blue come forth
> O Blue arise
> O Blue ascend
> O Blue come in (1994a, 3)

The repetition of "O Blue" suggests that a sacred ritual is taking place, and the capitalized "Blue" implies the name of a divine spirit. The ritual or prayer is performed at the birth of the boy, as a kind of baptism that does not wash away sins but instead provides the body with something sacred. At the same time, the passage could be read as an allusion to Plato's cave, with Blue as a particular boy's name. In this reading, the boy is being led from a world of illusion to a painful confrontation with light and truth, a confrontation that we accept as redeeming because of the sacred style of the language. Then, within the context of Jarman's *oeuvre*, one might read the passage as the young gay man being led out of the closet, experiencing a temporary pain but beginning a life of love and experience. In the passage the meanings of the words "You," "boy," light," and "Blue" can be interpreted as both transcendent and mundane, depending on the cultural frame the viewer uses.

In this work Jarman introduces the viewer to an overdetermined language that most of us, at least in everyday life, try to avoid in order to control meaning and limit misunderstanding. In particular, the opening passage provides an excellent example of how he uses the color blue to suggest multiple ways of desiring. Translated into a Lacanian vocabulary, *Blue* and the blue screen function as the *objet petit a*, the object-cause of desire.[8] The *objet petit a* is not a positive entity but an intangible element that raises the ordinary object to a sublime value. It is what causes us to love particular objects and people. And it is particularly insightful of Jarman to connect this element to a color, something that in itself has no substance but that coats other objects, creating a particular aura.

In typical Hollywood cinema, the power of the *objet a* is obscured through the use of fantasy. The evil villain is caught, and the film lets us believe that evil is confined to that particular villain. This alignment of object and fantasy provides temporary relief from the unknowability of the *objet a*. The traditional film thus presents a finite game (the detective wins by catching the villain) that tames the gaze by providing a definitive satisfaction. Jarman's proximity to death makes the pleasures of such a finite game less consoling. For example, he has seen that when one infection is fought off, another returns. Similarly, as a gay man he knows that society's conventional prizes do not necessarily satisfy. Instead, Jarman's work emphasizes that pleasure comes from what we *do* with objects and what we bring to them. By presenting viewers with the solid-blue screen, Jarman challenges them to create their own pleasure instead of adopting the fantasies of others.

However, that pleasure will not be a simple spiritual rebirth, as the opening passage might suggest. After the transcendent connotations of the opening, Jarman shifts to ordinary prose, focusing on the difficulties of daily life:

> I am sitting with some friends in this café drinking coffee served by young refugees from Bosnia. The war rages across the newspapers and through the ruined streets of Sarajevo.
>
> Tania said "Your clothes are on back to front and inside out." Since there were only two of us here I took them off and put them right then and there. I am always here before the doors open.
>
> What need of so much news from abroad while all that concerns either life or death is all transacting and at work within me. (1994a, 3)

While this is spoken, the screen changes from the ecstatic light of truth to a barrier to vision. We hear the sounds of the café and the weather outside, but we cannot see them; identifying with the speaking voice, the viewer is likely to experience the frustration of blindness. The passage emphasizes Jarman's marginal position in this world. Dressing oneself appropriately is a basic marker of socialization, and, because of his blindness, Jarman has difficulty performing this simple task. At the same time we see a diminished self-consciousness in his willingness to undress in the café. Social conventions have little value at this point in his life. Jarman also presents an atypical perspective on the war in Bosnia, conveying a frustration with this man-made conflict and acknowledging that his own illness demands a self-absorption that separates him from his peers. One might say that, for Jarman, Bosnia does not function as the gaze that draws his attention. He feels no need to imagine the motivations and desires of the war's participants. He is distracted by the gaze embodied in the HIV virus, that unknowable element that determines much of his daily life as well as his understanding of existence.

These first two sections present a pattern that continues throughout the film as Jarman moves back and forth between evocations of the transcendent and mundane events involving domestic events or medical procedures. The presence of the two different discourses limits the power of two standard illness fantasies: the fantasy of spiritual rebirth and the fantasy of restitution.[9] The fantasy of rebirth promises relief from the body through the soul; the fantasy of restitution offers victory over illness through willpower and determination. Jarman is forced by his illness to consider the mundane and the transcendent simultaneously, and he uses wit to bring enjoyment to this seemingly absurd situation when he exclaims: "The Gautama Buddha instructs me to walk away from illness./But he wasn't attached to a drip," (1994a, 9) and "If I lose half my sight will my vision be halved?" (7). What is striking about these jokes is that Jarman is able to frankly display the misery of his situation[10] along with an enjoyment of the new experiences, both physical and psychological, that this end passage brings.[11] Instead of demanding an overarching narrative that will make sense of everything, or looking for the magic potion that will return him to his previous life, Jarman commits to the present through the creation of this work of art. As a result, he is able to sustain limited, temporary desires that, paradoxically, allow some control over his failing body, the medical establishment, and the HIV virus.

We can see that this film, like most of Jarman's work, does not follow a linear conflict-leading-to-resolution structure but instead seeks to continually perpetuate desire in small increments.[12] One might say that he disregards the viewer's *comfort* in order to stimulate her *desire*. In *The Real Gaze: Film Theory after Lacan*, Todd McGowan presents a useful taxonomy for modern film with his categories "cinema of desire" and "cinema of fantasy." According to McGowan:

> The cinema of desire offers spectators the opportunity of recognizing and embracing their position as desiring subjects. It does not try to resolve desire through creating a fantasy scenario, but instead provides a filmic structure that reveals the impossibility of the *objet petit a*—the gaze—by depicting an absence in the visual field. By doing so, this type of cinema challenges the spectator in a way that typical Hollywood films do not. (2007, 70–71)[13]

If we place Jarman's films within the cinema of desire, the rationale behind many of his choices becomes clear. The commonsense understanding of desire is that it exists to be satisfied, but Lacan argues that, in fact, our goal is to perpetuate desire. Once a desired object is attained, satisfaction drains away from that object, and new objects must be found. This continuous dissatisfaction explains why the acceptance of a primordial lack (or castration) is central to the Lacanian worldview, and we see in both the form and content of Jarman's work a similar acceptance of lack and the consequent unwillingness to focus on one object of desire.[14] In Jarman's films the object of desire is not nearly as important as the imagination of the individual spectator, and this is why he offers so few resolutions and shows such impatience with attempts by others to circumscribe the desiring process.

His impatience becomes clear in several of his encounters with the medical and HIV/AIDS establishment, including a series of posters with question marks at the hospital: "HIV/AIDS?, AIDS?, HIV? ARE YOU AFFECTED BY HIV/AIDS? AIDS? ARC?, HIV?" (1994a, 27). The posters imply that a system is in place to treat HIV/AIDS as a problem with a clear solution. One need only ask, and one will receive answers. The illusion created by the posters is contradicted by Jarman's experience in the hospital, which is dominated by disorganization and uncertainty. Jarman is bothered by attempts to reduce AIDS to something simple and containable; or, one could say that he is frustrated with attempts to tame the gaze created by HIV with something as flimsy as a poster or pamphlet.

His impatience with finite solutions is further developed in his criticism of the AIDS quilt:

> I shall not win the battle against the virus—in spite of the slogans like "Living with AIDS." The virus was appropriated by the well—so we have to live with AIDS while they spread the quilt for the moths of Ithaca across the wine dark sea.
>
> Awareness is heightened by this, but something else is lost. A sense of reality drowned in theatre. (1994a, 9)

For Jarman, the problem with the AIDS quilt is that it shifts the focus from the pain and death of real people onto a clearly defined and controllable object. Making a quilt panel is a finishable project that provides satisfaction, and this is why Jarman sees it as theatre, or a kind of diverting game. Moreover, his allusions to Homer within the passage evoke Penelope at the loom, keeping herself busy to avoid the trauma of her missing husband and demanding suitors. The Homeric allusions remind us of the constant dismantling and reassembling of the AIDS quilt at different times and in new locations. This repetitive activity allows the healthy to feel like they are doing something, while people like Jarman continue to die. But most importantly, the quilt as spectacle replaces the image of the dying and dead. The public is able to avoid the trauma of death by focusing on the quilt, and thus the quilt itself tames the gaze. What do you want from me? I want you to make a panel for the AIDS quilt.

Of course one must not be too dismissive of the therapeutic and political efficacy of the AIDS quilt; my primary goal here is to contextualize Jarman's frustration. The paradox created by his critique is that his own film, which was shown in theatres, is also ostensibly a distraction and a form of entertainment. This paradox can be explained, however, if we go back to McGowan's distinction between the cinema of desire and the cinema of fantasy.[15] Clearly, if we look at fantasy as "the creation of possibility out of impossibility" (2007, 24), as McGowan suggests, then Jarman's work is thoroughly about imagining what the symbolic order excludes. Fantasy does appear in *Blue*; no film could function without it. But Jarman's goal is to create art that allows viewers, as much as possible, to desire in their own ways. He does this precisely by showing *too little*, by leaving room for the viewer's imagination. This gap, literalized in the solid-blue screen, necessarily limits Jarman's audience, because it creates dissatisfaction.[16] But Jarman shows us a way out of this dissatisfaction by presenting forms of enjoyment that have loosened their ties to the Other's desire. The payoff of Jarman's film is that when we separate from the fantasies of others, we are free to create our own fantasies, and this is precisely the traversal of fantasy that Lacan describes as the end of analysis.[17] The cinema of desire in Jarman's hands becomes a cinema of drive—a cinema of *jouissance*, or bliss.[18]

Blue's status as a film of bliss is confirmed by the rapturous poem with which it concludes. The poem is forty-four lines long and moves across time, between the living and the dead, and between the physical and the spiritual:

> Pearl fishers
> In azure seas
> Deep waters
> Washing the isle of the dead
> In coral harbours
> Amphora
>   Spill
>   Gold
> Across the still seabed
> We lie there
> Fanned by the billowing
> Sails of forgotten ships
> Tossed by the mournful winds
> Of the deep
> Lost Boys
> Sleep forever
> In a dear embrace
> Salt lips touching

In submarine gardens
Cool marble fingers
Touch an antique smile
Shell sounds
Whisper
Deep love drifting on the tide forever (1994a, 28–29)

The first section evokes the poetry of Sappho, with its short lines and references to islands, seas, and amphora, creating an important connection across time and culture. Jarman typically uses verse within *Blue* to detach from the domestic or medical spheres. Here he creates a space that is utopian but also sorrowful; it is full of feeling but also outside of time, mixing nature and culture. I do not want to over-analyze this poem, because my point is that Jarman presents images with which the imagination must play; his work does not fit neatly into an overarching framework. But the writing, particularly when spoken aloud on the sound track, draws attention to the materiality of the words and creates immediate feelings. For example, we feel the chiasmus of "Sails of forgotten ships," as well as the consonance in "Salt lips touching." Like other poets, Jarman uses these devices to slow the viewer down, to detach the words from their typical contexts, and to draw the viewer's attention to the pleasure of the signifier as well as the meaning of the signified.

Just as he draws on Sappho in this poem, Jarman also adapts passages from the apocryphal book of Wisdom, showing how one can make other discourses one's own. Here he describes his detachment from the finite games of conventional life and his new infinite perspective:

Our name will be forgotten
In time
No one will remember our work
Our life will pass like the traces of a cloud
And be scattered like
Mist that is chased by the
Rays of the sun
For our time is the passing of a shadow
And our lives will run like
Sparks through the stubble

I place a delphinium, Blue, upon your grave. (1994a, 30)

In this passage Jarman seems to discount the significance of life and work, but he conveys that insignificance with images of sublime beauty:

life is "Mist that is chased by/Rays of the sun." And although that beautiful mist is transient, it will continue to be seen throughout time, perhaps more easily by those who have seen Jarman's film. Jarman recognizes that the symbolic, represented by names and accomplishments, will lose meaning, but the Lacanian real, suggested by the beauty infusing the landscape, the love infusing human relationships, and the blue infusing the screen, endures.

The last line, "I place a delphinium, Blue, upon your grave" (in typical Jarman fashion), presents an ending that is still somewhat open. To whom do the pronouns refer? Is "Blue" a noun or an adjective? The ambiguity creates a space of identification for the viewer and a connection across time. We must all die ("*your* grave"), and we should all acknowledge the dead ("*I* place"), for our connections to the dead provide our actions with meaning. Just as Jarman uses Sappho and the unknown author of the book of Wisdom to comprehend his own situation, others will use Derek Jarman and the deaths of his generation to gain perspective on their own lives. One might argue that creating something beautiful is similar to placing a flower on a grave. As a gesture, it pays respect to those who have made things before us, and it also acknowledges our own mortality, leaving something for others.

By challenging his audience with the inevitable frustration of a static-blue screen, Jarman provides the viewer with a temporary proximity to blindness, disease, and the reality of death. But if the viewer has endured and worked with him, then something strange and wonderful will emerge. In what may be a summary of the film's goals, Jarman writes:

> In the pandemonium of image
> I present you with the universal Blue
> Blue an open door to soul
> An infinite possibility
> Becoming tangible. (1994a, 11)

In one way the film is a response to the bombardment of images we receive from popular culture, and it is also a response to distorting or manipulated images of people with AIDS. By temporarily stopping the proliferation of images, Jarman forces us to contemplate the real in the Lacanian sense: that which is infinite, intangible, and elusive and yet is constantly shaping our perceptions and our thinking. Unfortunately, the blue screen can only evoke the real if we have the vision to see it that way. The pleasure of desire must be stronger than the comfort of fantasy, the new plot more satisfying than the old.

Conclusion

The Genre of the Unconscious

Up until this point I have explored why particular authors have utilized the memoir genre near the end of their lives. My argument has been that a terminal illness diagnosis forces a change of view—from the finite to the infinite—that initiates a reinterpretation of the events of the author's past. Although proximity to death challenges the author's previous understanding of self and the world, it also provides an authority that allows the author to separate from established discourses, writing what he or she chooses regardless of form or convention. Thus the tone and style of these memoirs reflect a desire freed from the demands of both genre and propriety, and this freedom enables the reinterpretation of stories (the traversal of a fantasy) presented in the author's previous work. The reinterpretation (and thus the memoir) becomes essential to the process of finishing one's own story and reconfiguring the world and existence.

In this final chapter I add to this discussion of the motivation for writing memoirs an inquiry into the motivation for reading them, hopefully providing some insight into the late twentieth-century memoir boom. In a 2006 opinion piece in the *New York Times*, psychoanalyst Adam Phillips asserts that "psychotherapy turns up historically at the point at which traditional societies begin to break down and consumer capitalism begins to take hold." In the essay, he focuses on the ways in which culture manages the important aspects of life beyond human control: "gods and God, love and sexuality, mourning and amusement, character and inspiration, the past and the future." He suggests that tradition and religion previously guided us through these issues, and that the reification produced by consumer capitalism—the belief that the right product can provide happiness—actually hinders our ability to understand these intangible experiences. If psychotherapy has flourished in response to absence created by this confluence of cultural

developments, then I would argue that the demand and interest in the
memoir is a similar response to this gap.[1] Phillips acknowledges that
the arts have always played an important role in exploring metaphysical issues, but we also know that while some texts resonate across the
centuries, others lose resonance or "symbolic efficiency" because of
changes in cultural understandings of "truth" and "reality." Clearly,
the memoir gained symbolic efficiency throughout the 1980s and 1990s.
In 1996, James Atlas wrote in the *New York Times Magazine* that "the
triumph of memoir is now established fact," and one can now safely
say that the public's interest in the memoir appears to be the result
of specific cultural changes, and not a momentary trend.

In *The Art of Time in Memoir*, Sven Birkerts (2008) provides several insights into what makes a good memoir, and these insights can
help us better understand the social role of this genre. First, Birkerts
distinguishes the literary memoir from those autobiographies of states-
men or celebrities that follow a documented and shared historical
memory. He argues that, in contrast, the memoir follows what Proust
labeled involuntary memory (what Allon White called "the moments
and episodes which haunt or hurt" [1981, 3]) and therefore plays an
inherently "irrational" and subversive role:

> One of the distinguishing features of the dull and dutiful
> memoirs that crowd our display tables is that they measure
> all experience in terms of a standardized, or universalized,
> scale of values. . . . Coming face-to-face with the contradic-
> tion between what I felt should be important and what in
> fact *seemed* important, I could understand my project [his
> own memoir] as the attempted working out of a problem.
> Mainly: What did my so-called real memories add up to?
> What were they telling me that was different from the
> authorized version I had of my life? (2008, 9–10, emphasis
> in original)

We see in Birkerts's language a shift in the definition of reality. Following Freud's emphasis on the unconscious as the *primary* process,
Birkerts sees his involuntary memories as, in fact, his "real" memories. As a result, he uses the unconscious as his guide to revise truths
governed by the socially established norms and fantasies enforced by
the symbolic and the imaginary.

Another important feature Birkerts describes develops out of his
distinction between voluntary and involuntary memory (the dialectic
between "authorized" and unconscious discourses). Whereas the boring

memoir follows an "and then" structure, narrating events chronologically through linear cause-and-effect relationships, the literary memoir embraces a double vantage point that turns the text into an act in itself, shifting the emphasis from the past to the present:

> This manipulation of the double vantage point is the memoirist's single most powerful and adaptable technique, allowing for a complex temporal access. . . . The latter [the second, revisionist vantage point] counteracts the coma-inducing logic of, "If I just tell what happened. . . ." and promotes the dramatizing of the process of realization, which is the real point. (2008, 17)

Birkerts thus reinforces the point I made in Chapter 3 about the performative aspect of the memoir and how this differentiates it from the novel. The memoir is primarily a psychological quest, and while other genres may illustrate a similar quest, the memoir enthusiastically and unabashedly challenges Aristotle's convention of developing character through action by minimizing the action *inside* of the narrative and shifting the emphasis to the extradiegetic act of writing itself. The quest is performed, not described, and the meta-narrative becomes more important than the narrative. In addition, the reflexive meta-narrative creates the impression that the author is speaking directly to the reader, reinforcing the memoir's aura of truth.

Thus my point is that the literary memoir, at its best and in its modern form, is a genre rooted in the exploration of the unconscious and could really only fully develop once Freud's revolutionary emphasis on the unconscious gained widespread acceptance (i.e., gained its own symbolic efficiency). Any writing based on the unconscious works much better when connected and constrained by "real" experience. Lacan teaches that the unconscious is structured like a language, a structure that makes the memoirist's search possible. The unconscious is not, however, a culturally established discourse. Although certain types of anxiety dreams (arriving at an exam unprepared; finding oneself naked in public) are shared by many people, the decoding of specific elements of the unconscious requires a personal knowledge that is unavailable to us, which accounts for our interest in our own dreams and our boredom with the dreams of other people. Indeed, the separateness of unconscious fantasy is discussed explicitly by Freud in "The Poet and Daydreaming": "You will remember that we said the day-dreamer hid his phantasies carefully from other people because he had reason to be ashamed of them. I may now add that even if he were to communicate them to us, he would give us no pleasure by his disclosure. When we hear such phantasies they repel us, or at least leave us cold" (1958, 53). He explains that the writer transforms this raw material so it becomes entertaining for the reader, and that this aesthetic transformation is the essence of the poet's art. Freud suggests that the writer "softens the egotistical character of the day-dream by changes and disguises, and he bribes us by the offer of a purely formal, that is, aesthetic, pleasure in the presentation of his phantasies" (1958, 54). The poet thus overcomes the barriers between our individual unconscious discourses by translating his experience into a common, socially acceptable language.[2]

Like the poet, the memoirist (at least the successful memoirist) translates experience into a socially acceptable language and, as I argued in Chapter 1, the kind of language that is deemed acceptable changed dramatically in the twentieth century. Although we are now less likely to be repelled by personal disclosures, we may still be left cold by the impenetrable signifiers of someone's unconscious. The memoirist differs from the poet in that she or he uses the double vantage point to solve this problem. At the beginning of the text the signifiers are just as impenetrable to the author as they are to the reader: the dynamic of the memoir is the quest to dialectize these problematic signifiers, placing them into a broader narrative that provides them with meaning (if not necessarily absolute truth). It is in this quest that the memoir resembles the therapeutic process. Therefore, the main attraction of the memoir is the method of discovery, not the events or signifiers themselves, and this is why a successful memoir can be written by someone without prominent status or cultural success. As a genre of the unconscious, the memoir illustrates how the unconscious can be accessed, and how this access enables understanding of the intangible aspects of existence described by Phillips. Birkerts explains that in "reading their work, we borrow their investigative energy and contemplate similar ways of accessing our own lives" (2008, 22). The memoir therefore reflects the modern belief that, in Richard Rorty's words, we now see "every human life as a poem" (1989, 35), a poem that is discovered and composed in a dialectical process made familiar by both therapy and the memoir.

My goal here has been to show how an encounter with radical contingency such as a terminal illness diagnosis destroys particular fantasies and provokes a rewriting of one's life from the position of unknowingness or death. The accomplishment of this particular kind of rewriting, the separation from the structures and fantasies that give our lives meaning, is a heroic accomplishment, and that aura of heroism is another important draw of the memoir. In his discussion of Nietzsche and Harold Bloom in *Contingency, Irony, and Solidarity*, Rorty argues that to fail as a "poet" is to accept "somebody else's description of oneself" (1989, 28). He explains that because, for many people, modern culture provides no clear justification for one's existence, that justification comes in the creativity with which one leads one's life, a creativity that is always in tension with an imaginary ego that prefers the security of stasis. Psychoanalysis as theorized by Lacan envisions a similar encounter with contingency and the same use of this encounter with meaninglessness in order to rewrite the self based precisely on the drive that the void has freed from the restraining ego. Within the Lacanian paradigm, we all become poets, at least in the Nietzschean/Bloomian vocabulary that Rorty employs:

> Only poets, Nietzsche suspected, can truly appreciate contingency. The rest of us are doomed to remain philosophers, to insist that there is really only one true lading-list, one true description of the human situation, one universal context of our lives. We are doomed to spend our conscious lives trying to escape from contingency rather than, like the strong poet, acknowledging and appropriating contingency. (1989, 28)

Thus the analysand who finishes his or her analysis and qualifies as an analyst moves from the position of philosopher to that of poet. To identify with the symptom, to move from desire to drive, to traverse the fantasy, and to go through the Pass are ways of describing the momentary feeling that one is not a replica being written by the discourses of others. By giving birth to oneself, by placing *Ich* where *Es* was, the analyst privileges freedom over security, and this is why so many authors of terminal illness memoirs express a surprising joy and energy after the initial shock of the diagnosis wears off. After this traversal they were able to, in Bruce Fink's phrase, "enjoy their enjoyment."[3] And I quote Rorty's description of the move from philosopher to poet because his language ties together the two parts of this project, the artist and the analyst, and reveals their similarity. Clearly, one of the most frustrating aspects of reading Lacan's texts is the shifting nature of the terms he employs. But what Lacan is trying to do is avoid the position of the philosopher—the possessor of the one true lading list—and he does this by performing the position of the poet, by constantly redescribing his ideas in a new vocabulary. This frustration created by Lacan's shifting terms is countered, however, by the enjoyment presented in the seminars themselves. We hear in Lacan's writings the *jouissance* of the performance, and this attracts us and, as with the memoir, "we borrow this investigative energy." This insistence on a new vocabulary transforms his knowledge, just as these authors have transformed their experience, from descriptions into acts.

Lacan emphasized that the subject performing the work of analysis is the *analysand*, not the analyst. The analyst can punctuate the analysand's speech in order to lead her to look at her life in new ways, but in the end the knowledge must come from the analysand through her own work. This emphasis on self-creation also explains why the analysand decides when the analysis is finished. Only she knows when the opaque spots have been deciphered; the analyst does not have access to that knowledge. Therefore, the analysand is responsible for the final terms of judgment, and this is, I argue, a particularly postmodern quality that psychoanalysis shares with the memoir. Inherent in the memoir form is the construction of its own terms of judgment; the author examines himself as protagonist within the text and evaluates his own thoughts and behavior. In this way, the memoir is a prime example of the self-legitimating "little narrative" described by J.-F. Lyotard. In addition, this reflexivity leads to inherently postmodern qualities such as the celebration of difference and uncertainty and a willingness to embrace ruptures that more traditional forms of literature exclude or resolve. The subjective quality that once made the memoir marginal and unseemly is now, in fact, the source of its relevance.

Notes

Chapter 1

1. Thomas Couser argues, persuasively in my view, that the rise of the illness memoir has resulted from the confluence of two trends: "One is the destigmatization of illness and disability, which such narratives at once reflect and seek to advance. Another is the extension of identity politics to illness" (1997, 8). The connection between the two is particularly clear in texts labeled "testimony" or "witnessing" that connote "speaking truth to power."

2. "The place where cultural experience is located is in the potential space between the individual and the environment (originally the object). The same can be said of playing. Cultural experience begins with creative living first manifested in play" (Winnicott 1971, 100). In *Playing and Reality* (1971), see "Transitional Objects and Transitional Phenomena," "The Use of an Object and Relating through Identifications," and "The Location of Cultural Experience."

3. As well as pages 102–19 in *Truth and Method* (2004), see Gadamer, "On the Problem of Self-Understanding" (1976) in *Philosophical Hermeneutics*.

4. Croce's article has become a frequently cited source for the "high art" position against personal and political art. She has become such a familiar whipping "person" that it seems almost necessary to thank her for stating this position with such vehemence and abandon.

5. For more information on Jones and "Still/Here," see Bill Jones (1995), *Last Night on Earth*; Henry Louis Gates, "The Body Politic: Choreographer Bill T. Jones," *The New Yorker* 70:39 (November 28, 1994): 112; *Bill T. Jones: Still/Here with Bill Moyers*. Dir. David Grubin. PBS, 1997.

6. A similar interpretation is presented by Jacques Lacan (2006) in "The Function and Field of Speech and Language in Psychoanalysis," in *Ecrits*, 319/262.

7. This leads to Lacan's assertion in "Position of the Unconscious" that "every drive is virtually a death drive," *Ecrits*, 848/719.

8. I realize that my taxonomy has the unusual effect of placing Arlene Croce and Paul Monette in the same category, even though they would clearly despise each other's work. Some justification for this pairing appears, however, in Monette's frequent engagement with critics in *Becoming a Man* and *Last*

Watch of the Night (in particular see the essay "Getting Covered"). Monette, like Croce, cares about critics. Contrast this with Harold Brodkey (1996), who, in *This Wild Darkness*, writes: "It was a relief to get away from the tease and rank of imputed greatness and from the denial and attacks and from my own sense of things, of worldly reality and of literary reality—all of it" (38).

9. The rise of fundamentalism throughout the world can be viewed as a parallel reaction to a perceived failure of "nature" and "tradition."

10. John Rajchman (1991) emphasizes the significance of Seminar VII in his *Truth and Eros*: "This is what Lacan told his Seminar in 1972; these are the first words of his *Encore*. They suggest that the Seminar on Ethics, the only one he wanted to write up as a book, enjoyed a special place in his oeuvre; he would have continued along his singular path, his *cheminement*, just because he would never be able to be done with it" (29).

11. In *Culture and the Real* (2005), Catherine Belsey provides a thorough and lucid reading of the beautiful and sublime in Lacan's Seminar VII. My reading is indebted to Belsey's insight.

12. Kathryn Harrison's 1997 memoir of incest, *The Kiss*, provides a useful example, as responses to the book varied from extreme praise to virulent condemnation.

13. See Winnett (1990, 505–18).

14. See Fink, *The Lacanian Subject* (1995), and *A Clinical Introduction to Lacanian Psychoanalysis* (1997).

15. See Butler (2005, 20).

16. "Finally, though Žižek does give examples of subjects who act ethically (i.e., in accordance with the dictates of the drive) from within the horizon of fantasy, there is next to nothing concerning the subject of the drive (i.e., the subject who emerges on the 'other' side of fantasy), and—most urgently—the implications this carries for the very possibility of community" Daly (2001, 103). Bruce Fink (1997), in *A Clinical Introduction to Lacanian Psychoanalysis*, writes, "Lacan gives us only a few examples of people who act as one might after traversing one's fundamental fantasy and freeing the drives from their inhibitions" (277).

Chapter 2

1. "Too Close to the Bone" was published simultaneously in Britain and the United States in the *London Review of Books*, May 4, 1989, and *Raritan* 8 (Spring 1989); it is reprinted in White's (1993) *Carnival, Hysteria, and Writing: Collected Essays and Autobiography*. "Why Am I a Literary Critic?" was written in 1984 and first published in *Carnival, Hysteria, and Writing*.

2. Lacan (1992) develops the concept of the Thing (*das Ding, la Chose*) in his Seminar VII, *The Ethics of Psychoanalysis*. Sarah Kay (2003) provides a concise summary of the concept in her Žižekian glossary: "The Thing, for Lacan, is the point just outside the scope of symbolization where the sense that the symbolic has a limit concentrates itself into a threat of what might

lie beyond that limit. The Thing is, in language, what the blind spot is in our vision: it can be present in its very absence, as the point from which some invisible menace threatens. At the point of the Thing, the drives, especially the death drive, seem to press upon us" (172).

3. The "beast upon the shore" is clearly an allusion to Virginia Woolf's (1931) *The Waves*, to which White refers later in the essay.

Chapter 3

1. As Ellie Ragland (1995) explains: "However, nothing less than the death of ego certainties can enable a person to reconstruct his or her being around new desire. For the alienations that anchor one in fixed identifications are based on the fear of loss. People settle for any known set of identifications, however painful, lest they fall out of the familiar symbolic order into the real of anxiety which opens onto a void of actual emptiness at the center of being" (94).

2. In the university discourse, knowledge (S2) occupies the position of agent, placing jouissance (*a*) in the position of other, producing an alienated subject ($) who finds truth in a new master signifier (S1):

$$\frac{S2}{S1} \qquad \frac{a}{\$}$$

3. Lacan presents the master discourse as

$$\frac{S1}{\$} \qquad \frac{S2}{a}$$

This provides the basic matrix for the other three discourses. As Žižek explains, in the master discourse "a subject is represented by the signifier for another signifier (for the chain or the field of 'ordinary' signifiers); the remainder—the 'bone in the throat'—that resists this symbolic representation, emerges (is "produced") as *objet petit a*, and the subject endeavors to 'normalize' his relationship toward this excess via fantasmatic formations (which is why the lower level of the formula of the Master's discourse renders the matheme of fantasy $<>a)" (1998 75–76).

4. "Yet, by disqualifying universal notions of justice, freedom, and the good, for being inveterately 'metaphysical,' for colonising and suppressing their others with the violence consequent on the chimera of correspondence, 'post-modernism' has no imagination for its own implied ground of justice, freedom and the good. This ground is therefore held in a transcendence far off the ground, where, with a mixture of naivity and cynicism, without reason and in despair, post-modernism leaves analysed and unanalysed according to its tenets the pre-conditions and rampant consequences of power, domination, and authority" (Rose 1996, 7).

5. "Yet this glimpsed unified world is nevertheless purely formal; the antagonistic nature of the inner and outer worlds is not abolished but only recognised as necessary; the subject which recognises it as such is just as empirical—just as much part of the outside world, confined in its own interiority—as the characters which have become its objects" (Lukacs 1971, 75).

6. Bruce Fink summarizes the structure of the hysteric's discourse

$$\frac{\$}{a} \qquad \frac{S1}{S2}$$

"In the hysteric's discourse, the split subject occupies the dominant position and addresses S1, calling it into question. . . . In the lower right-hand corner, we find knowledge (S2). This position is also the one where Lacan situates jouissance, the pleasure produced by a discourse, and he thus suggests here that an hysteric gets off on knowledge. . . . object *a* appears in the position of truth. That means that the truth of the hysteric's discourse, its hidden motor force, is . . . commanded by the real, that is, by that which does not work, by that which does not fit" (1995, 133–35).

7. See, in particular, *The Ticklish Subject* (Žižek 1999a, 369–77), "From Phallus to the Act."

8. "The Real here is precisely that missed opportunity: the trauma of betrayal, of what might have been. The alternative history fantasy of what might have happened is not simply an illusion, but functions as a betrayal or haunting of the Real" (Žižek and Daly 2003, 102).

9. For a discussion of the depiction of the diseased as Other, see Sander Gilman (1988), *Disease and Representation: Images of Illness from Madness to AIDS*.

10. Lorenzo Chiesa's (2007) reading of Seminar VII is particular useful here, in that he makes explicit how Antigone's actions are a direct response to Creon's refusal of a lack in the law: "Antigone deliberately embraces 'second death'—symbolic death—only in order to resist the *hybris* of Creon's law, his 'excessive,' unreasonable decision to condemn Polynices' dead body to a second death. Antigone does not cede on her suicidal demand to bury Polynices because this is the only way in which she can make *desire* appear; in showing the void of pure desire through her splendor, she 'saves' desire from Creon's strictly speaking totalitarian attempt to obliterate the Real-of-the-Symbolic, the lack of the law, through the imposition of an (impossible) universal good turned into a 'criminal' good" (178–79, emphasis in original).

11. "Counsel woven into the fabric of real life is wisdom" (Benjamin 1968, 86–87).

Chapter 4

1. See "His Own Best Construction" (Menaker 1996), and "A Genius for Publicity" (Bawer 1988).

2. Brodkey was diagnosed in 1993, before the successful development of protease inhibitors.

3. Brodkey announced that he had AIDS in an article entitled "To My Readers," which appeared on June 21, 1993, in *The New Yorker*. Most of that article and the one that followed, "Dying: An Update" (February 7, 1994), are incorporated into the memoir *This Wild Darkness: The Story of My Death*, posthumously published in 1996.

4. On the Pass, see Fink (1997, 213); Dunand (1995, 251–56); Roudinesco (1997) and Schneiderman (1983, passim).

5. Elizabeth Bruss provides a helpful explanation of the contractual nature of autobiography's definition: "The generic 'force' of autobiography and the leading features that have distinguished it throughout its history from other kinds of discourse are contextual rather than formal. There is no narrative sequence, no stipulated length, no metrical pattern, and no style that is unique to autobiography or sufficient to set it apart from biography or even fiction. To count as autobiography a text must have a certain implicit situation, a particular relationship to other texts and to the scene of its enactment. Three parameters define this situation and give classical autobiography its peculiar generic value:

> Truth value. An autobiography purports to be consistent with other evidence; we are conventionally invited to compare it with other documents that describe the same events (to determine its veracity) and with anything the author may have said or written on other occasions (to determine its sincerity).
>
> Act-value. Autobiography is a personal performance, an action that exemplifies the character of the agent responsible for that action and how it is performed.
>
> Identity-value. In autobiography, the logically distinct roles of author, narrator, and protagonist are conjoined, with the same individual occupying a position both in the context, the associated "scene of writing," and within the text itself" (Bruss 1980, 296–320).

6. Einat Avrahami (2003) uses the scholarship of Diana E. H. Russell to make the important point that "Brodkey's self-myth of irresistibility—which sustains his tacit belief that he in fact seduced his stepfather and subsequent abusers—is not unique but rather shared by many other abused children who were sexually assaulted within the family" (172, n. 186–87).

7. At different points Brodkey speculates that his lack of affection for his birth mother and adoptive parents robbed them of their will to live: "I was told that Doris took me once to the hospital to see my mother, who smelled of infection and medicines and that I refused her embrace, clinging instead to the perfumed Doris; the rescued child was apparently without memory of the dying mother. (Perhaps that was the real crime, and not my obduracy with Joe.)" (1996, 94–95).

8. "I have never, since childhood, really expected to be comforted" (Brodkey 1996, 36). I have accepted since childhood the transience of everything, including meaning—poor orphan that I was" (1996, 137).

9. According to Dinitia Smith of the *New York Times*: "The novel had many titles, including 'Party of Animals.' For years the book appeared in the Farrar, Straus & Giroux catalogue only to be withdrawn. At one point, four Farrar Strauss employees were spending weekends typing Mr. Brodkey's revisions in what they referred to as a 'Party of Typing.' 'Publishing would interfere with working on it,' Mr. Brodkey said to a reporter about the novel" (1996, 11).

10. A familiar example of interpassivity is the committed fan who works tirelessly to promote and monitor an actor or athlete. The fan selects the celebrity to enjoy on his or her behalf, while the fan simply chronicles the celebrity's activities.

11. "Subversion of the subject and dialectic of desire," in *Ecrits* (2006, 299–300), and Seminar XI (1978, 44–45).

12. "And I felt that if I had AIDS, she had the right, perhaps the duty, to leave me; my having that disease suspended all contracts and emotions—it was beyond sacrament and marriage. It represented a new state, in which, in a sense, we did not exist" (Brodkey 1996, 15).

13. See Lacan's essay, "Desire and the Interpretation of Desire in *Hamlet*" in Felman (1982).

14. "In his earlier books, this technique, combined with a seeming reluctance to edit out even the most trivial, abstruse remark, often resulted in windy, self-indulgent narratives that were solipsistic to the point of parody" (Kakutani 1996).

15. See K. R. Eisler (1971), *Discourse on Hamlet and Hamlet: A Psychoanalytic Inquiry*; Tamise Van Pelt (2000), "The Discourse of Desire and the Resisters in Hamlet," in her *The Other Side of Desire*; Bruce Fink (1996), "Reading Hamlet with Lacan"; and Freud's (1965) comments in *The Interpretation of Dreams*.

16. Richard Boothby explains Lacan's use of this term to describe the liminal feeling that comes with the recognition of fantasy ($<>a$): "It is perhaps most with the *objet a* in mind that Lacan coined the phrase "extimate." It is something of the subject's own, indeed, the most intimate part, yet it always appears elsewhere, outside the subject and eluding its grasp" (2001, 243).

17. "Toward the end of my experience of homosexuality, before I met Ellen, I underwent the most outrageous banishment to a role of sheer, domineering, hatred and worshipped masculinity" (Brodkey 1996, 30).

18. "My outer life often feels that the dramas and exertions of order, the emergencies and efforts of imagination of this inner Manhattan are shortening that outer life. And have ruined it and are ruining it more. For me to work seems reckless and lonely, peninsular" (1999, 326).

19. The variable definitions of traversing the fantasy and the Pass are also discussed by Žižek in "The Undergrowth of Enjoyment," in Wright and Wright (1999, 32).

20. "Because of the peculiar circumstances of my life I had to find a way to get along with my conscious mind, or I really couldn't exist, and one way to do that was to start thinking about my life as a story, or something to be interpreted or examined" (Linville 1991, 60).

Chapter 5

1. To whom Jarman paid tribute in his short film *Imagining October*.

2. As Bruce Fink explains, "While existence is granted only through the symbolic order (the alienated subject being assigned a place therein), being is supplied only by cleaving to the real" (1995, 61).

3. To follow the mirror-stage analogy, Jarman assumes the place of the parent holding the child, thus occupying the position of ideal ego: "I have described elsewhere the sight in the mirror of the ego ideal, of that being that he first saw appearing in the form of the parent holding him up before the mirror. By clinging to the reference-point of him who looks at him in a mirror, the subject sees appearing, not his ego ideal, but his ideal ego, that point at which he desires to gratify himself in himself" (Lacan 1978, 257).

4. Included in *Reading for the Plot* (Brooks 1984).

5. Klein is famous for his monochrome paintings using IKB, or International Klein Blue.

6. As a small sample of responses to the film, here are two reviews cited by Roland Wymer (2005, 174): "It [*Blue*] gives you the freedom to flee if you wish. . . . But finally you do not want to escape. . . . And the imagery—that pool of colour that beckons and absorbs your attention and then absorbs it rebaptised, re-sensitised—is too pliant, too precious to be resisted by any filmgoer brought up on the rude unchanging colours of commercial cinema" (Nigel Andrews in the *Financial Times*). " 'Watching' becomes a rather different experience, at once active and passive. You work to make sense: to assimilate this rather demanding experience and perhaps even to stay awake. But you also accept that your own attention will fade in and out, as your associations take you elsewhere. That drifting vision is an inescapable part of watching *Blue*" (Jonathan Romney in *New Statesman and Society*, qtd. in Wymer 2005, 174). Finally, Paul Julian Smith writes, "Jarman's *tabula rasa* shows how in all cinema vision is distorted by sound: we read the blue screen according to prompts from the soundtrack as now the storm of the epidemic; now heaven 'seen without looking out of the window'; now the 'fathomless blue of bliss' " (1993, 19).

7. See, in particular, *The Sublime Object of Ideology*, chapter 3, "*Che Vuoi?*" 87–130 (Žižek 1989).

8. "*The* objet a *in the field of the visible is the gaze*" (Lacan 1978, 105), emphases in original).

9. For more on the myth of rebirth see Hawkins (1999, 31–60). For more on the restitution narrative see Frank (1995, 75–96).

10. "The illness knocks you for six/Just as you start to forget it/A bullet in the back of the head/Might be easier" (1994a, 26).

11. One might argue that the film itself is a response to the experience of the medical treatment of his eyes: "The shattering bright light of the eye specialist's camera leaves that empty sky blue after-image" (1994a, 27). The blue afterimage caused by the doctor becomes the screen of the film.

12. All of Jarman's films have a static quality (usually attributed to his background as a painter) that comes from his frequent use of tableau and montage. Therefore, even when Jarman uses images, he abandons cinematic and narrative conventions that would "naturalize" meaning.

13. McGowan's (2007) *The Real Gaze* is a modern manifesto for a new Lacanian film theory, building on recent scholarship by Joan Copjec and Slavoj Žižek. McGowan explains how early film theorists such as Christian Metz and Laura Mulvey misinterpreted Lacan's theory of the gaze as the action of looking, a misinterpretation that developed out of an overreliance on Lacan's early "Mirror Stage" essay. McGowan shows that for the later Lacan, the gaze comes from the *object*, not from the person looking. It is that element that attracts the viewer's eye and pulls her into a network of meanings. My analysis of the gaze in *Blue* is indebted to his clarification of this concept.

14. Paul Julian Smith describes *Blue* as a "hymn to love" (1993, 18), and one might argue that Jarman posits love as a supreme good, but love is never confined to one object. For example, Jarman's partner, Keith Collins (H. B.), has an important but a limited role in his autobiographical works.

15. McGowan (2007) provides a useful shorthand to these concepts with his chapter titles. The cinema of fantasy shows too much, while the cinema of desire does not show enough. He is careful to point out, however, that the cinema of fantasy is equally capable of disturbing the status quo through its revelations, in that it "confronts spectators with the sources of their own enjoyment and deprives them of the illusion of a neutral social reality" (2007, 25).

16. McGowan (2007) explains that the cinema of desire is often an unpopular cinema, because "to experience the cinema of desire is to experience what one doesn't have" (2007, 71).

17. "We can now see why the maxim of psychoanalytic ethics as formulated by Lacan ('not to give way on one's desire') coincides with the closing moment of the psychoanalytic process, the 'going through the fantasy': the desire with regard to which we must not 'give way' is not the desire supported by fantasy but the desire of the Other beyond fantasy" (Žižek 1989, 118).

18. "Bliss" was the original title for *Blue*. See Peake (1999, 398).

Conclusion

1. A similar explanation can be found in the scholars of "Reflexive Modernization," such as Ulrich Beck, Anthony Giddens, and Scott Lash, who

suggest that the waning of belief in tradition and nature has created a constant self-monitoring and reliance on expert systems, two important aspects of the memoir's inherently reflexive function. See, in particular, Beck's (1991) *Risk Society*, Giddens's (1991) *Modernity and Self-Identity*, and Lash and Urry's (2002) *Economies of Signs and Space*.

2. An illustrative example is Allon White's explanation of the missing Bernoulli meter from his novel *Gifts*, discussed earlier: "Last week it suddenly occurred to me as so obvious that it made me laugh out loud. Throughout my youth I had listened, day after day, to a single lament from my father: why hadn't the – – – arrived from Bedford yet?" (1993, 55). The ordinary reader has no way of interpreting the idiosyncrasies of White's displacement: it is raw and undisguised.

3. "One of my analysands expressed the neurotic's predicament quite nicely by saying that he could not 'enjoy his enjoyment,' implying that his satisfaction was, in some sense, ruined or tainted by simultaneous feelings of dissatisfaction or displeasure. Perhaps one way of stating the configuration analysis aims at is to say that *the analysand is at last allowed to be able to enjoy his or her enjoyment* (Fink 1997, 210–11, emphasis in original).

Works Cited

Apollon, Willy, and Richard Feldstein, Eds. 1996. *Lacan, Politics, Aesthetics.* Albany: State University of New York Press.

Atlas, James. 1996. "The Age of the Literary Memoir Is Now." *New York Times Magazine*, May 12, 25–27.

Avrahami, Einat. 2003. "Impacts of Truth(s): The Confessional Mode in Harold Brodkey's Illness Autobiography." *Literature and Medicine* 22:2 (Fall): 164–87.

Bawer, Bruce. 1998. "A Genius for Publicity." *The New Criterion* (December): 58–69.

Beck, Ulrich. 1991. *Risk Society: Towards a New Modernity.* Translated by Mark Ritter. London: Sage.

Belsey, Catherine. 2005. *Culture and the Real.* London: Routledge.

Benjamin, Walter. 1968 [1955]. "The Storyteller: Reflections on the Work of Nikolai Leskov." In *Illuminations*, ed. Hannah Arendt, 83–110. New York: Schocken Books.

Bill T. Jones: Still/Here with Bill Moyers. 1997. Dir. David Grubin. P85.

Birkerts, Sven. 2008. *The Art of Time in Memoir.* St. Paul, MN: Graywolf Press.

Bloom, Harold. 1982. *Agon: Towards a Theory of Revisionism.* Oxford: Oxford University Press.

Boothby, Richard. 2001. *Freud as Philosopher.* London: Routledge.

Bracher, Mark. 1993. *Lacan, Discourse, and Social Change.* Ithaca, NY: Cornell University Press.

Bradbury, Malcolm, and James McFarlane. 1976. *Modernism: A Guide to European Literature 1890–1930.* New York: Penguin Books.

Brodkey, Harold. 1989. *Stories in an Almost Classical Mode.* New York: Vintage-Random House.

———. 1991. "The Art of Fiction CXXVI." *Paris Review* 121: 51–91.

———. 1992. *The Runaway Soul.* New York: Harper Collins.

———. 1993. "To My Readers." *New Yorker* (June 21): 80–82.

———. 1994. "Dying: An Update." *New Yorker* (February 7): 70–84.

———. 1996. *This Wild Darkness: The Story of My Death.* New York: Metropolitan-Henry Holt.

———. 1999. *Sea Battles on Dry Land.* New York: Metropolitan-Henry Holt.

Brooks, Peter. 1984. *Reading for the Plot*. Cambridge, MA: Harvard University Press.

Brophy, Sarah. 2004. *Witnessing AIDS: Writing, Testimony, and the Work of Mourning*. Toronto: University of Toronto Press.

Bruss, Elizabeth W. 1980. "Eye for I: Making and Unmaking Autobiography in Film." In *Autobiography: Essays Theoretical and Critical*, ed. James Olney, 296–320. Princeton, NJ: Princeton University Press.

Butler, Rex. 2005. *Slavoj Zizek: Live Theory*. London: Continuum.

Carse, James P. 1986. *Finite and Infinite Games: A Vision of Life as Play and Possibility*. New York: The Free Press.

Chambers, Ross. 1998. *Facing It: AIDS Diaries and the Death of the Author*. Ann Arbor: University of Michigan Press.

———. 2004. *Untimely Interventions: AIDS Writing, Testimonial, & the Rhetoric of Haunting*. Ann Arbor: University of Michigan Press.

Chiesa, Lorenzo. 2007. *Subjectivity and Otherness: A Philosophical Reading of Lacan*. Cambridge, MA: MIT Press.

Collard, Cyril. 1993. *Savage Nights*. Translated by William Rodarmor. London: Quartet Books.

Cook, Matt. 1996. "Derek Jarman's Written Work." In *Derek Jarman: A Portrait*, 105–11. London: Thames and Hudson.

Couser, G. Thomas. 1997. *Recovering Bodies: Illness, Disability, and Life Writing*. Madison: University of Wisconsin Press.

Croce, Arlene. 1994."Discussing the Undiscussable." *New Yorker* (December 26): 54–60.

Daly, Glyn. 2001. " 'There Is no Other of the Other' Symptoms of a Decline in Symbolic Faith, or, Zizek's Anti-Captialism." *Paragraph* 24:2 (July): 79–110.

De Man, Paul. 1979. "Autobiography as De-facement." *MLN* 94: 919–30.

Derek Jarman: A Portrait. 1996. London: Thames and Hudson.

Dolan, J. D. 1996. "Twilight of the Idol." *The Nation* 25 (March): 35–36.

Dollimore, Jonathan. 1995. "Sex and Death." *Textual Practice* 9:1: 27–53.

Dunand, Anne. 1995. "The End of Analysis (II)." In *Reading Seminar XI*, ed. Feldstein, et al., 251–58. Albany: State University of New York Press.

Eakin, Paul John. 1985. *Fictions in Autobiography*. Princeton, NJ: Princeton University Press.

Edelman, Lee. 1993. "The Mirror and the Tank: 'AIDS,' Subjectivity, and the Rhetoric of Activism." In *Writing AIDS*, ed. Timothey Murphy and S. Poirier, 9–38. New York: Columbia University Press.

Egan, Susanna. 1999. *Mirror Talk: Genres of Crisis in Contemporary Autobiography*. Chapel Hill: University of North Carolina Press.

Eisenstein, Sergei. 1949. *Film Form*. Translated and edited by Jay Leyda. New York: Harvest/HBJ.

Eissler, K. R. 1971. *Discourse on Hamlet and Hamlet: A Psychoanalytic Inquiry*. New York: International University Press.

Elliott, Anthony. 2002. *Psychoanalytic Theory: An Introduction*. 2nd ed. Durham, NC: Duke University Press.

Feldstein, Richard, Bruce Fink, and Maire Jaanus, eds., 1995. *Reading Seminar XI.* Albany: State University of New York Press.

Felman, Shoshana, ed. 1982. *Literature and Psychoanalysis.* Baltimore, MD: Johns Hopkins University Press.

Fink, Bruce. 1995. *The Lacanian Subject.* Princeton, NJ: Princeton University Press.

———. 1996. "Reading Hamlet with Lacan." In *Lacan, Politics, Aesthetics,* ed. Apollon and Feldstein, 181–98. Albany: State University of New York Press.

———. 1997. *A Clinical Introduction to Lacanian Psychoanalysis.* Cambridge, MA: Harvard University Press.

Fish, Stanley. 1999. "Just Published: Minutiae without Meaning." *New York Times,* September 7, A19.

Foster, Dennis. 1997. *Confession and Complicity in Narrative.* Cambridge: Cambridge University Press.

Frank, Arthur. 1995. *The Wounded Storyteller: Body, Illness, and Ethics.* Chicago, IL: University of Chicago Press.

Freud, Sigmund. 1958. "The Poet and Daydreaming." In *On Creativity and the Unconscious,* ed. Benjamin Nelson, 44–54. New York: Harper and Row.

———. 1959. *Inhibitions, Symptoms, and Anxiety.* Edited by James Strachey. New York: Norton.

———. 1960. *The Ego and the Id.* Edited by James Strachey. New York: Norton.

———. 1961. *Beyond the Pleasure Principle.* Edited by James Strachey. New York: Norton.

———. 1963. *Character and Culture.* Edited by Philip Rieff. New York: Collier Books.

———. 1965. *The Interpretation of Dreams.* Edited by James Strachey. New York: Avon Books.

Gadamer, Hans-Georg. 1976. "On the Problem of Self-Understanding" (1962). In *Philosophical Hermeneutics,* ed. and trans. David E. Linge, 44–58. Berkeley: University of California Press.

———. 2004. *Truth and Method.* Translated by Weinsheimer and Marshall. London: Continuum.

Gates, Henry Louis. 1994. "The Body Politic: Choreographer Bill T. Jones," *The New Yorker,* 70:39, November 28.

Giddens, Anthony. 1991. *Modernity and Self-Identity: Self and Society in the Modern Age.* Stanford, CA: Stanford University Press.

Gilman, Sander. 1988. *Disease and Representation: Images of Illness from Madness to AIDS.* Ithaca, NY: Cornell University Press.

Griffin, Susan. 1992. *A Chorus of Stones: The Private Life of War.* New York: Doubleday.

Guibert, Hervé. 1991. *To the Friend Who Did Not Save My Life.* Translated by Linda Coverdale. New York: Atheneum.

Harrison, Kathryn. 1997. *The Kiss.* New York: Avon Books.

Heath, Stephen. 1981. *Questions of Cinema.* Bloomington: Indiana University Press.

Hunsaker Hawkins, Anne. 1999. *Reconstructing Illness: Studies in Pathography*. West Layfayette, IN: Purdue University Press,.

Jaanus, Maire. 1995. "The Demontage of the Drive." In *Reading Seminar XI*, ed. Feldstein, Fink, and Jaanus, 119–36. Albany: State University of New York Press.

Jameson, Fredric. 1971. *Marxism and Form*. Princeton, NJ: Princeton University Press.

———. 1988. "The Imaginary and Symbolic in Lacan (1977)." In *The Ideologies of Theory Essays 1971–1986 Volume 1: Situations of Theory*, 75–115. Minneapolis: University of Minnesota Press.

Jarman, Derek. 1987. *The Last of England*. London: Constable.

———. 1993a [1992]. *At Your Own Risk: A Saints Testament*. Woodstock, NY: The Overlook Press.

———. 1993b [1984]. *Dancing Ledge*. Woodstock, NY: The Overlook Press.

———. 1994a [1993]. *Blue: Text of a Film by Derk Jarman*. Woodstock, NY: The Overlook Press.

———. 1994b [1991]. *Modern Nature*. Woodstock, NY: The Overlook Press.

Jones, Bill T. 1995. *Last Night on Earth*. New York: Pantheon.

Kakutani, Michiko. 1996. "This Wild Darkness." *New York Times*, December 24.

Kay, Sarah. 2003. *Zizek: A Critical Introduction*. Cambridge: Polity.

Kermode, Frank. 1967. *The Sense of an Ending: Studies in the Theory of Fiction*. Oxford: Oxford University Press.

Kramer, Larry. 1994. *Reports from the Holocaust: The Story of an AIDS Activist*. New York: St. Martin's Press.

———. 2000. *The Normal Heart* and *The Destiny of Me*. New York: Grove Press.

Lacan, Jacques. 1978. *Seminar XI: The Four Fundamental Concepts of Psycho-Analysis*. Edited by Jacques-Alain Miller. Translated by Alan Sheridan. New York: Norton.

———. 1982. "Desire and the Interpretation of Desire in *Hamlet*." In *Literature and Psychoanalysis*, ed. Shoshanan Felman, 11–52. Translated by James Hulbert. Baltimore. MD: Johns Hopkins University Press.

———. 1991 [1975]. *The Seminar of Jacques Lacan: Book I: Freud's Papers on Technique*. Edited by Jacques-Alain Miller. Translated by John Forrester. New York: Norton.

———. 1992. *The Seminar of Jacques Lacan: Book VII: The Ethics of Psychoanalysis*. Edited by Jacques-Alain Miller. Translated by Dennis Porter. New York: Norton.

———. 1993 [1981]. *The Seminar of Jacques Lacan: Book III: The Psychoses*. Edited by Jacques-Alain Miller. Translated by Russell Grigg. New York: Norton.

———. 2006. *Ecrits*. Translated by Bruce Fink. New York: Norton.

———. 2007. *The Seminar of Jacques Lacan: Book XVII: The Other Side of Psychoanalysis*. Edited by Jacques-Alain Miller. Translated by Russell Grigg. New York: Norton.

Laplanche J., and J.-B. Pontalis. 1973. *The Language of Psycho-Analysis*. Translated by Donald Nicholson-Smith. New York: Norton.

Lash, Scott, and John Urry. 2002 [1994]. *Economies of Signs and Space*. London: Sage.

Linville, James. 1991. "Harold Brodkey: The Art of Fiction." *Paris Review* 121: 50–91.

Lorde, Audre. 1982. *Zami: A New Spelling of My Name*. Freedom, CA: The Crossing Press.

———. 1984. *Sister/Outsider*. Freedom, CA: The Crossing Press.

———. 1988. *A Burst of Light*. Ithaca, NY: Firebrand Books.

Lukacs, Georg. 1971 [1920]. *The Theory of the Novel*. Translated by Anna Bostock. Cambridge: MIT Press.

Lyotard, Jean-Francois. 1984. *The Postmodern Condition: A Report on Knowledge*. Translated by Geoff Bennington and Brian Massumi. Minneapolis: University of Minnesota Press.

McGowan, Todd. 2007. *The Real Gaze: Film Theory after Lacan*. Albany: State University of New York Press.

Mellard, James. 2006. *Beyond Lacan*. Albany: State University of New York Press.

Menaker, Daniel. 1996. "His Own Best Construction." *New York Times Book Review* (February 25): 35.

Miller, Nancy K. 1994. "Representing Others: Gender and Subjects of Autobiography." *differences* 6:1: 1–27.

Monette, Paul. 1992. *Becoming a Man: Half a Life Story*. New York: Harcourt Brace Jovanovich.

———. 1988. *Borrowed Time: An AIDS Memoir*. New York: Avon Books.

Nash, Mark. 1994. "Chronicle(s) of a Death Foretold, Notes Apropos of *Les Nuit Fauves*." *Critical Quarterly* 36:1: 97–104.

Olney, James. 1972. *Metaphors of Self*. Princeton, NJ: Princeton University Press.

———, ed. 1980. *Autobiography: Essays Theoretical and Critical*. Princeton, NJ: Princeton University Press.

Peake, Tony. 1999. *Derek Jarman's Biography*. Woodstock, NY: Overlook Press.

Phillips, Adam. 2000. *Darwin's Worms: On Life and Death Stories*. London: Basic Books-Faber and Faber.

———. 2006. "A Mind Is a Terrible Thing to Measure." *New York Times*, February 26.

Potter, Dennis. 1994. *Seeing the Blossom: Two Interviews and a Lecture*. London: Faber and Faber.

Ragland, Ellie. 1995. *Essays on the Pleasure of Death*. New York: Routledge.

Ragland-Sullivan, Ellie. 1987. *Jacques Lacan and the Philosophy of Psychoanalysis*. Urbana: University of Illinois Press.

Rajchman, John. 1991. *Truth and Eros: Foucault, Lacan, and the Question of Ethics*. London: Routledge.

Restuccia, Frances L. 2006. *Amorous Acts: Lacanian Ethics in Modernism, Film, and Queer Theory*. Stanford, CA: Stanford University Press.

Rorty, Richard. 1989. *Contingency, Irony, and Solidarity.* Cambridge: Cambridge University Press.

Rose, Gillian. 1993. *Judaism and Modernity: Philosophical Essays.* Oxford: Blackwell Publishers.

———. 1995a. *Hegel: Contra Sociology.* 2nd ed. London: Athlone.

———. 1995b. *Love's Work: a Reckoning with Life.* New York: Schocken Books.

———. 1996. *Mourning Becomes the Law.* Cambridge: Cambridge University Press.

———. 1999. *Paradiso.* London: The Menard Press.

Rose, Jacqueline. 1993. "Afterword." In *Carnival, Hysteria, and Writing: Collected Essays and Autobiography.* Allon White, 178–86. Oxford: Clarendon Press.

Roudinesco, Elisabeth. 1997. *Jacques Lacan.* Translated by Barbara Bray. New York: Columbia University Press.

Schneiderman, Stuart. 1983. *Jacques Lacan: The Death of an Intellectual Hero.* Cambridge, MA: Harvard University Press.

Schwenger, Peter. 1996. "Derek Jarman and the Color of the Mind's Eye." *University of Toronto Quarterly* 65:2 (Spring): 419–26.

Shakespeare, William. 1982. *Hamlet.* Edited by Harold Jenkins. London: Methuen Arden Shakespeare.

Silverman, Kaja. 1992. *Male Subjectivity at the Margins.* New York: Routledge.

Smith, Dinitia. 1996. "Harold Brodkey, 65, New Yorker Writer and Novelist, Dies of Illness He Wrote About." *New York Times,* January 27, 11.

Smith, Paul Julian. 1993. "Blue and the Outer Limits." *Sight and Sound* (June): 18–21.

Soler, Colette. 2003. "The paradoxes of the symptom in psychoanalysis." In *The Cambridge Companion to Lacan.* Edited by Jean-Michel Rabaté. Cambridge: Cambridge University Press.

Sontag, Susan. 1990. *Illness as Metaphor and AIDS and Its Metaphors.* New York: Anchor-Doubleday.

Sprinker, Michael. 1980. "Fictions of the Self: The End of Autobiography." In *Autobiography: Essays Theoretical and Critical,* ed. James Olney, 321–42. Princeton, NJ: Princeton University Press.

Stallybrass, Peter, and Allon White. 1986. *The Politics of Poetics of Transgression.* Ithaca, NY: Cornell University Press.

Thurston, Luke, ed. 2002. *Re-Inventing the Symptom.* New York: Other Press.

Van Pelt, Tamise. 2000. *The Other Side of Desire: Lacan's Theory of the Registers.* Albany: State University of New York Press.

Verhaeghe, Paul. 2001. *Beyond Gender: From Subject to Drive.* New York: Other Press.

Verhaeghe, Paul, and Frederic Declercq. 2002. "Lacan's Analytic Goal: *Le sinthome* or the Feminine Way." In *Re-Inventing the Symptom,* ed. Luke Thurston, 59–82. New York: Other Press.

Watney, Simon. 1989. *Taking Liberties: AIDS and Cultural Politics.* New York: Serpent's Tail.

———. 1993. "The French Connection." *Sight and Sound* (June): 24–25.

White, Allon. 1981. *The Uses of Obscurity: The Fiction of Early Modernism*. London: Routledge.

———. 1993. *Carnival, Hysteria, and Writing: Collected Essays and Autobiography*. Oxford: Clarendon Press.

Winnett, Susan. 1990. "Coming Unstrung: Women, Men, Narrative, and Principles of Pleasure." *PMLA* 105:3 (May): 505–18.

Winnicott, D. W. 1971. *Playing and Reality*. London: Tavistock/Routledge.

Wright, Elizabeth, and Edmond Wright, eds. 1999. *The Zizek Reader*. Oxford: Blackwell, 11–36.

Woolf, Virginia. 1931. *The Waves*. New York: Harcourt Brace.

Wymer, Roland. 2005. *Derek Jarman*. Manchester: Manchester University Press.

Žižek, Slavoj. 1989. *The Sublime Object of Ideology*. London: Verso.

———. 1992. *Looking Awry*. Cambridge, MA: MIT Press.

———. 1997. *The Plague of Fantasies*. London: Verso.

———. 1998. "Four Discourses, Four Subjects." In *Cogito and the Unconscious*, ed. Slavoj Žižek, 74–113. Durham, NC: Duke University Press.

———. 1999a. *The Ticklish Subject*. London: Verso.

———. 1999b. "The Undergrowth of Enjoyment." In *The Žižek Reader*, ed. Elizabeth Wright and Edmond Wright, 11–36. Oxford: Blackwell.

Žižek, Slavoj, ed. 1998. *Cogito and the Unconscious*. Durham, NC: Duke University Press.

Žižek, Slavoj, Judith Butler, and Ernesto Laclau. 2000. *Contingency, Hegemony, Universality: Contemporary Dialogues on the Left*. London: Verso.

Žižek, Slavoj, and Glyn Daly. 2003. *Conversations with Zizek*. Cambridge: Polity Press.

Index